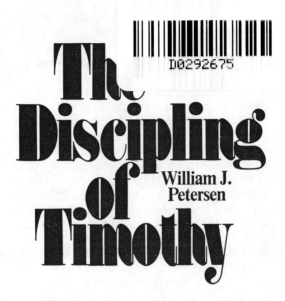

The Discipling of Timothy

William J. Petersen

While this book is designed for the reader's personal profit and enjoyment, it is also intended for group study. A Leader's Guide with Victor Multiuse Transparency Masters is available from your local bookstore or from the publisher.

VICTOR BOOKS

a division of SP Publications, Inc.

WHEATON, ILLINOIS 60187

Offices also in Fullerton, California • Whitby, Ontario, Canada • Amersham-on-the-Hill, Bucks, England

Cover art by Kurt Dietsch

Recommended Dewey Decimal Classification: 229:092
Suggested Subject Heading: BIBLE—BIOGRAPHY

Library of Congress Catalog Card Number: 80-50002
ISBN: 0-88207-217-x

VICTOR BOOKS
A division of SP Publications, Inc.
P.O. Box 1825 • Wheaton, Illinois 60187

CONTENTS

Why Timothy?

A fuzzy-cheeked youth scared of his shadow. . . . Isn't that the stereotype you have of Timothy?

An indomitable spirit who ran roughshod over anyone or anything that slowed him down in his quest to bring the Gospel to the world. . . . Isn't that the picture you have of Paul?

Then how in the world did these two get together? For many reasons it looked like a big mistake. It was one of those alliances that shouldn't have worked out. Yet it did.

I wouldn't be at all surprised if Timothy at many points in his life wondered, "What am I doing here?" or thought, "I said 'Yes' once too often," or "The job is 10 times as big as I am."

It's easy to understand why God chose Paul, an educated Jew with Roman citizenship, and from a city steeped in Greek culture. He was the ideal man to take the Gospel to Athens and Rome, the ideal man to witness to both Jews and Gentiles.

But why Timothy? He came from a small mountain

town, perhaps the smallest, most rural, most uncultured community that Paul visited. Timothy was not particularly healthy nor did he impress people with his authority. If Timothy had an inferiority complex, there was good reason for it.

Paul once wrote to the Corinthians, those rough and ready citizens of the seaport city, "Now if Timothy comes, see that he is with you without cause to be afraid; for he is doing the Lord's work, as I also am. Let no one therefore despise him" (1 Cor. 16:10-11, NASB). Timothy hardly seemed to be a fitting emissary for the intrepid Apostle Paul.

Why Timothy? Was it really a mistake to choose Timothy? Would the Gospel have been spread farther and faster during the first century if Paul had chosen someone else instead of that young lad from Lystra?

Hardly. God knew what He was doing. And God knows what He is doing today when He puts you into positions of opportunity and responsibility that seem to be too much for you. You may feel that you've been shoved out of the boat and told to wade to shore when the water's 10 feet deep. You're in over your head.

Well, if you've ever had a Timothy complex, it's good to see how that youthful sidekick of Paul coped with a job that was more than he could handle.

The Beginning of Timothy's Story

Let's go back more than 1,900 years to the middle of the first century. The year was about A.D. 47, 17 years after the death, burial, resurrection, and ascension of Jesus Christ. The Christian church, then, was 17 years old. Paul himself would have been around 45 years old, and a Christian for the past 14 years.

Paul had been working in the church in Antioch. This progressive, growing city, located 300 miles north of

Jerusalem, had become the third largest metropolis in the Roman Empire, with a half million residents (the size of Atlanta, Denver, or Pittsburgh).

Antioch was also the gateway to the West, and the church in Antioch was composed of men and women who had come from various parts of the Roman Empire. Among them were Paul and Barnabas. Paul had come from Tarsus which was about 100 miles to the northwest, and Barnabas was a native of the island of Cyprus, a boat ride of 100 miles to the southwest.

So the church in Antioch, led by the Holy Spirit to extend Christianity westward, selected Barnabas and Paul to be their first missionaries. Barnabas, probably in his mid-50s, had been a wealthy landowner on Cyprus before his conversion. Paul, some 10 years younger, had been trained as a Jewish rabbi. With these two went John Mark, who was about 30 years old. Since he was Barnabas' nephew, John Mark would have been somewhat familiar with the island of Cyprus.

The first stop of the missionary trio was Cyprus, as might be expected. Then after sweeping through Cyprus, the trio sailed northward to what is now called Turkey and stopped briefly at Perga, a little city slightly inland.

It was here that John Mark quit. Instead of staying with his Uncle Barnabas and Paul, Mark headed back to Antioch. No one knows exactly why. Maybe even Paul didn't understand why, and the loss of his helper was obviously a bitter pill for him to swallow. If Mark had been a teenager, the blame might have been charged to homesickness or health. But he was no teenager and was certainly more robust in health than Paul. Perhaps there was something in the hinterlands of Asia Minor that frightened Mark.

This is what faced the missionary troupe: The southern coast of Turkey had no major cities and was infested with pirates. The lowlands along the coast were also infested with mosquitoes, which were often more dangerous than the pirates since they bore malaria. Sir William Ramsay, a 19th-century Bible scholar, thought that Paul himself had caught malaria in the lowlands around Perga (see Gal. 4:13). That may have been why Paul and Barnabas quickly ventured inland, up and into the highland plain where Antioch of Pisidia lay. While the mountains were not infested with pirates and mosquitoes, they were controlled by robber bands that the Roman army had difficulty subduing. Paul may have had the Taurus Mountains in mind when he spoke of "perils of robbers" (2 Cor. 11:26).

Whether John Mark feared the malaria of the lowlands, the robbers of the highlands, or the uncivilized barbarians of the inland cities is not known. Perhaps he simply felt that the missionary tour should have ended in Cyprus; his job description didn't call for him to go farther.

However, Barnabas and Paul continued the tour. It was another 100-mile trek to Pisidian Antioch, which was a key city on the great Eastern trade route from Ephesus to the Euphrates River. A major cosmopolitan community with a significant Jewish population, Antioch opened up briefly to the Gospel message and a church was born. But opposition came quickly, and Paul and Barnabas had to move on.

The next stop was Iconium, about 80 miles to the southeast. F.F. Bruce in *Paul: Apostle of the Heart Set Free* calls the experience of Paul and Barnabas in Iconium "almost a carbon copy of that in Pisidian Antioch" (Eerdmans, p. 166). There was a riot, and the two missionaries were about to be stoned. Hastily, they fled across the border to a small town in the province of Lycaonia, about 18 miles from Iconium. The border town was Lystra, in which the teenager Timothy lived.

It doesn't seem as though Lystra had been in Paul's game plan. It was not a big town, nor was it influential in the territory. Besides that, the Jewish population was small and most of the residents spoke in a Lycaonian dialect, not Greek. The *Wycliffe Historical Geography of Bible Lands* puts it this way: "The site was off the main roads, and its seclusion marked it out as a small rustic town, where the people and customs would be quite provincial." Though once "a place of some importance," it was now sinking "into the insignificance of a small provincial town" (Moody, p. 351).

Disappointed by his apprentice John Mark who had quit on him, ravaged by malaria or some other disease, evicted from Pisidian Antioch, and practically stoned in Iconium, Paul walked through the city gate of the secluded mountain town of Lystra.

God expects us to plan, as Paul and Barnabas did. It is not wrong to have a strategy, a plan of action. But the mark of the mature Christian is what he does when the plan is scuttled.

At this point, no one would have blamed Paul and Barnabas if they had said, "That's enough for one missionary trip. Let's rest here for a few days and then head for home." But Paul and Barnabas felt that God must have something else for them to do; He had a purpose in their being in this forsaken country town called Lystra.

That's how Paul got to Lystra. How Timothy got there is another story.

Timothy's Family

Timothy's mother was named Eunice, and his grandmother, Lois. His father's name is not given, but he is identified as being a Greek. So there they were, a Greek husband and a Jewish wife in a Lycaonian town.

Eunice's Jewish ancestors may have been living there for as many as 250 years. It had been about that long before that the Greek ruler Antiochus had encouraged thousands of Jews to emigrate from Babylonia to Asia Minor. Jews were given the most favored citizen status and soon became leaders in commerce and business throughout the region. That's why Paul and Barnabas found so many Jews in most of the inland cities of the area.

About 6 B.C., the Roman Emperor Augustus, perturbed by the unruly nature of the Lycaonian natives, declared the frontier town of Lystra a Roman colony and brought in Roman troops and Greek merchants to try to civilize the area. Perhaps Timothy's Greek father came about that time.

As a result, the population of Lystra was diverse, including Roman officials and soldiers, although with each decade, Rome's interest in Lystra was waning. The Greek or Hellenic residents were among the town's VIPs. The Jewish population was small. It only took 10 Jewish families to establish a synagogue, but there was no synagogue in Lystra, unlike nearby Iconium.

The bulk of the population, however, was the native Lycaonian stock—emotional, competitive, and superstitious. Most of the residents spoke Greek in public, but in their homes they easily lapsed into their native dialect.

Timothy came from a home divided both religiously and nationally. The fact that his mother married a Greek is not surprising. The farther from Jerusalem, the less rigid were the Jews in following the ban on intermarriage.

In the Greek culture of the time, morality seemed in short supply. Those who were appalled by the cultural drift admired the standards of the Jews. As a result, quite a few Greeks became proselytes of the Jewish religion, and many more who didn't want to go that far became secret admirers of Judaism.

Where Timothy's father stood is unknown. He certainly didn't prevent his wife from instructing their son in the Scriptures (2 Tim. 3:14-15). Nor did he interfere with his son being named Timotheus, which literally means "honoring God" or "dear to God." The name itself was Greek, and this must have satisfied the father; the meaning of the name must have satisfied the mother.

The father, however, hadn't allowed Timothy to be circumcised (Acts 16:1-3), so he obviously wasn't a proselyte or even a secret admirer of his wife's faith. Perhaps he, like many in the Greek world of that day, was fed up with religion. William Barclay in *Train Up a Child* says, "In the case of the Greeks it was not that men became so depraved that they abandoned their gods, but that the gods became so depraved that they were abandoned by men" (Westminster, p. 202).

Timothy's father would not have been among the rabble that welcomed Paul and Barnabas into Lystra as though they were gods returned from Mount Olympus. Rather, he may have welcomed the educated Jews into his home and engaged them in a philosophical discussion, in the same way that the Athenians welcomed Paul on Mars Hill. And after the evening was ended, he would have sent Paul and Barnabas away with the words, "We will hear thee again on this matter."

(Since the Scripture does not record anything more about Timothy's father, it is also possible that he had recently died, leaving the teenaged boy, his mother, and grandmother to fend for themselves in the Gentile city of Lystra.)

Timothy's Training

Timothy's education was remarkable. Paul commended

the quality of the instruction that Timothy had received (2 Tim. 1:5; 3:14-15); but to be honest, compared with the Ivy League training that Paul had enjoyed, Timothy's education was second-rate. Paul was born to Hebrew parents and had no doubt been schooled in a reputable synagogue in the university of Tarsus, before traveling to Jerusalem as a teenager to sit at the feet of Gamaliel, the foremost Jewish educator of the day.

Timothy, on the other hand, came from a divided home, lived in a rustic community with no synagogue, and may never have traveled farther than 30 miles from home. Yet Paul commended Timothy's education.

Why? Because the Jews recognized that the center of true education was not the synagogue, but the home. "In no other religion," wrote Isidore Epstein in *The Jewish Way of Life,* "has the duty of parents to instruct their children been more stressed than in Judaism."

Certainly synagogues aided parents in their duty to educate. But there was no way around it; it was still the parents' responsibility to instruct their children whether there was a synagogue in town or not.

Besides that, it was the wife's responsibility as well as the husband's. Frequent references were made in Old Testament passages to both father and mother. At the beginning of the Book of Proverbs, for instance, Solomon wrote, "My son, hear the inspiration of thy father, and forsake not the law of thy mother" (1:8). And the last chapter of the book (see 31:1) is the actual instruction of a mother to her son, who happened to be King Lemuel.

Early in the Gospel of Luke, there are words of praise from Mary, the mother of Jesus (Luke 1:28, 36-56), and almost every phrase is a reference to an Old Testament passage. It is obvious that she not only knew the Scripture well but was also prepared to pass on instruction in the Scriptures to her children.

This was not so in Greek society where, Barclay says, "The Athenian mother was unequipped to be of any help to her child in the matter of education" (*Train Up a Child*, p. 91). She herself was uneducated. Perhaps this was one reason why Paul had to limit the role of women in Greek churches.

The Jews—male and female alike—were known as "people of the Book," the Scripture. It wasn't that everyone possessed a copy of the Bible in his home—but that everyone possessed the Bible in his heart.

The focus of Jewish education was God's Word; there was no other textbook but the Scriptures. Beginning at age three or four, the Jewish children were educated in the Old Testament, and education in that day meant memorization. Children learned by rote, repeating aloud after the teacher, until they could repeat entire passages.

When children learned to read (and literacy among Hebrew children was extremely high), they learned from the Scriptures.

Study was not the quiet process that it is in schools today where students read silently. An old Jewish saying admonished students: "Study not only with the eyes, but with the eyes and the mouth." As Jewish young people studied, they were urged to repeat aloud the Scriptures they were reading.

In Lystra, Timothy may never have seen a Scripture scroll, but his mother Eunice was a walking, talking scroll, his living Scripture. Years later when Paul wrote his second epistle to Timothy, he reminded him to stick with the Scriptures, because Timothy knew from whom he had learned them. (See 2 Tim. 3:14.) That's the added dimension of parental instruction. Eunice not only taught the Scriptures to her son, but she lived their truths before her son. Years later Paul could remind Timothy not only to remember the instruction, but also to remember the godly example of the one from whom he had learned it.

Today the father's role is stressed in evangelical circles, and properly so; but, like Eunice, many mothers must take the responsibility for the spiritual training of their children. Perhaps the father is not a Christian or the mother must rear the children alone.

In the midst of a poor environment, is it possible to rear a child in the fear of the Lord?

Well, Eunice did it. Fellowship with God's people was meager; the heathen society surrounded them. The father's spiritual indifference must have placed a heavy burden on Eunice, but God sustained her.

When Timothy is first mentioned (Acts 16), he must have been in his mid-to-late teens. There probably had been no bar mitzvah for him in Lystra, when he entered teenage years and became a man. In fact, Eunice might well have been concerned about this. Perhaps she worried that she had sheltered him too much from the heathen influences of Lystra. Single parents often have those fears. Perhaps without a Jewish father, he had become too much a mama's boy. Eunice may have felt he needed the example of a strong male figure in his life, a rabbi perhaps, who could show him that it wasn't being a sissy to live for Jehovah. Perhaps.

Paul and Barnabas

Then came the two visitors through the city gates. Just outside those city gates was the temple to Zeus. No one could get near Lystra without noticing it. It was Lystra's main claim to fame, as far as the native population was concerned.

According to an old legend, the gods Zeus and Hermes once visited that region and no one recognized them. No one even gave them a place to stay. No one, that is, except two old peasants, Philemon and his wife Baucis. This elderly couple took them in and were kind to them.

As a result, so the old myth goes, the whole population except for Philemon and Baucis was wiped out, and Philemon and Baucis were made the guardians of a splendid temple. When the elderly couple died, they were turned into two great trees.

Naturally, the superstitious townsfolk didn't want that to happen again. The temple to Zeus outside their gates served notice that the gods were welcome in Lystra. No doubt there were two trees planted there, symbolizing Philemon and Baucis.

The Hellenes in town, like Timothy's father, probably ignored this old myth. But the native population took no chances.

And then came the two visitors to town.

Of course, Paul and Barnabas weren't thinking about Zeus and Hermes when they approached Lystra. They were fleeing from Iconium where they had been almost stoned. Normally, it was a six-hour journey; probably they made it in less time. Lystra was a Roman colony, and to Paul and Barnabas, that meant law and order.

And besides, it was another city where they could share the good news that God had visited this planet and had brought salvation through Jesus Christ.

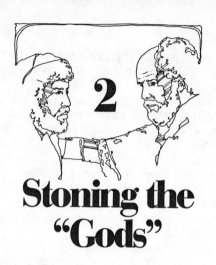

2

Stoning the "Gods"

"He was a man of low stature, bald (or shaved) on the head, crooked thighs, handsome legs, hollow-eyed, had a crooked nose; full of grace; for sometimes he appeared as a man, sometimes he had the countenance of an angel."

That is a supposed description of the Apostle Paul, taken from a second-century, somewhat spurious, apocryphal writing called *The Acts of Paul and Thecla* (chap. 1, v. 7). What makes it interesting is that Thecla is said to have lived in Iconium, only 18 miles from Timothy's hometown of Lystra. The description is supposedly of Paul as he entered the town of Lystra.

While parts of the story of Thecla are far-fetched, other parts seem to bear some marks of authenticity; and it is possible, as some scholars affirm, that the description of Paul may be reasonably accurate.

Probably, at this point, Paul didn't care how he looked. He had escaped the stone-throwing mobs at Iconium, and still struggled with what was most likely a malarial attack. Exhausted from the 18-mile hike, Paul no doubt sought lodging first of all.

I doubt if Paul and Barnabas were noticed as they passed by the temple of Zeus outside the city and then slipped through the city gates. The gates would have been crowded with townsfolk chatting with one another, peddlers hawking their wares, and the ever-present beggars pleading for money.

I would have looked for a Holiday Inn, but Paul's practice was to look for a synagogue because he could be sure to find Jewish families living nearby. Since Lystra had no synagogue, Paul and Barnabas asked directions to any Jewish homes in the area. This was the pattern that Paul followed wherever he went. In Philippi where there was no synagogue, Paul found women in a prayer meeting by the riverside, and one of the women, Lydia, invited them to stay at her home.

Where Paul stayed in Lystra is not known, but with the Jewish community as small as it was, Timothy's household would have known about Paul's arrival. Not too many Jewish rabbis made their way through Lystra, so Paul and Barnabas would have been welcomed as honored guests by the small Jewish population.

Most people in Paul's situation would have tried to lie low for awhile and recuperate. After nearly being stoned in both Pisidian Antioch and Iconium, Paul should have taken it easy in Lystra. After all, Iconium was only 18 miles away, and news traveled fast.

Preaching in Lystra

If Paul and Barnabas wanted excuses for a breather, they had plenty: Lystra had no synagogue to preach in; the natives spoke a foreign language; Paul was under the weather. But not only did they bring the Gospel to Lystra—they kept on preaching the Gospel throughout the area (Acts 14:6-7). The implication is that since

Lystra had no synagogue, Paul and Barnabas preached outdoors, probably near the city gates where the towns-folk congregated (Acts 14:8-9). And that would mean near the imposing temple of Zeus.

To Eunice and her son Timothy, this bold preaching must have seemed novel and maybe even brash. Jews did not normally evangelize. They taught their families, but they didn't go out on the street corners to preach. Gentiles sometimes were attracted to synagogue worship by the high moral standards of the Jews, but not by their preaching.

Most scholars feel that Timothy's mother Eunice became a Christian during the early days of Paul's visit here. Maybe Timothy and his grandmother did also. In the first Letter to Timothy, Paul addressed him as "my own son in the faith," (1:2) and it seems probable that the apostle personally led the lad to a saving knowledge of Jesus Christ.

Paul and Barnabas had a reckless enthusiasm in spreading their faith, and this must have made a deep impression on the somewhat shy Timothy. Did God expect him to do what Paul and Barnabas were doing? That would be expecting too much. That would be a greater responsibility than he could bear.

How long Paul and Barnabas preached the Gospel in Lystra and the surrounding area is not known, but some commentators feel the evangelistic work may have been quite extensive. The language barrier, however, may have kept the two missionaries from having great success, for although the bilingual Lycaonians understood Greek, they somewhat resented it. But to a teenager named Timothy, whose first language was Greek, those must have been exciting days.

There was someone else in Lystra who was also much impressed by Paul's preaching. He was a cripple, and must have been badly deformed. Dr. Luke called him "impotent in his feet." In Greek medical usage, the word for *impotent* referred to incurable cases. Oftentimes the same word is translated "impossible" (Matt. 19:26, NASB). The man was also said to have been "a cripple from his mother's womb." And then as if Luke hadn't made his point, he added, "who never had walked." Obviously, the man was a hopeless case, well-known to all the citizenry.

As he sat daily by the city gates, the cripple may have heard news from Iconium, how Paul and Barnabas had worked miracles there. And if indeed Paul preached regularly by the city gates, this cripple had more opportunity to hear the Gospel than anyone else. In spite of the language barrier, the cripple perceived enough of the message to believe.

As Paul preached one day, he noticed the man. No doubt, he had seen the cripple before; but this time Paul saw not only the man, but also his faith. And Paul said loudly, "Stand upright on your feet," (Acts 14:10, NASB) in the same manner that Jesus had cried with a loud voice at the tomb of Lazarus. In neither case was it necessary to shout to get the attention of the one who would be the beneficiary of the miracle, but rather to get the attention of the people milling around.

The word that Paul used for "upright" is the Greek word *orthos* from which we have our word "orthopedics." Incidentally, the vivid language used in this story indicates to A.T. Robertson, a noted Southern Baptist New Testament scholar, that Luke got the story directly from Timothy himself who had witnessed the miracle (*Word Pictures in the New Testament,* Broadman).

Obviously, however, Timothy wasn't the only witness. The townspeople were there too.

The townspeople no doubt were startled by Paul's

bold command to the cripple, and they must have stopped and waited to see what would happen. They didn't have long to wait.

The cripple leaped up and began walking around. The English word *peripatetic* (taken directly from the Greek word used in this passage) means one who is constantly moving around. And that describes this ex-cripple. A lifetime of pent-up activity had suddenly been released.

The more that he leaped about, the louder came the shouts of the people. And as the shouts increased, the shopkeepers must have emerged from their stalls; nearby residents must have poked their heads out of their doors to see what the commotion was all about.

Zeus and Hermes

The townspeople may have been slow to understand the Greek of Paul and Barnabas, but they could understand a miracle. Now, the two missionaries had trouble understanding the shouts of the crowds. Moreover, Paul and Barnabas couldn't address the people at all in the uproar. The ruckus was intense and showed no signs of abating. Timothy, however, had no trouble understanding the shouts of the crowd: "The gods are come down in the likeness of men." The people thought that Barnabas and Paul were their gods Zeus and Hermes. These would correspond to Jupiter and Mercury in Roman mythology.

Whether Paul and Barnabas remained in the middle of the throng is unknown. Most likely, they got away and went to the residence where they were staying.

My guess is that Timothy would have stayed around to see what would develop. You see, he would have known why the people had compared Paul and Barnabas with the gods.

Remember the old myth mentioned in the first chapter? The story has also been immortalized by the Roman writer Ovid in *Metamorphoses*. Townspeople always wondered when the gods might drop in on them again.

The poet Homer wrote:

For in similitude of strangers oft
The gods who can with ease all shapes assume,
Repair to populous cities, where they mark
Th' outrageous and the righteous deeds of men.

According to tradition, Barnabas was a tall, dignified, and handsome man, a fitting image in which Zeus might reappear. Paul, on the other hand, was short and literally "the leader of the talk." Hermes was the messenger of the gods. He was said to have presided over orators, and was known, among other things, as the god of eloquence. We get our word *hermeneutics,* which has to do with the art of preaching, from his name.

It all seemed so logical to the people. They had a temple to Zeus at the gate of the city. Two strangers had come and had performed an incredible miracle. How could this be explained except by the appearance of Zeus and Hermes? Later, in writing to these people, Paul referred to the fact that they had received him as an angel of God (Gal. 4:14).

The priest, who normally prepared sacrifices of bullocks at the altar in front of the temple of Zeus, felt that this was the opportune time to prepare another sacrifice. In the past, the priest had always offered the sacrifice in front of Zeus' statue. This time, he would have the honor of offering it in front of Zeus in the flesh.

Whether the priest summoned Barnabas and Paul to the occasion or whether someone like Timothy ran to tell them first is not known. But the two men came to the crowd by the gate of the city and quickly ruined the festivities. By rending their clothes, they showed to the crowd that they were deeply distressed by the goings-on. It was as if the people were committing blasphemy. (See the action of the high priest in Matt. 26:65.)

A Young Looker-On

My guess is that Timothy was watching everything, taking it all in. Nothing like this had happened in Lystra during his lifetime, and he didn't want to miss anything.

While we're not sure what life had been like for Timothy, growing up in Lystra, we do know there was no open persecution of the Jews. Yet he was certainly conscious that he was one of a minority group, whether he identified with the Jewishness of his mother or the Hellenism of his father.

He didn't belong. The native Lystrans resented the religious exclusivism of the Jews and the cultural intrusion of the Hellenes. Timothy was a stranger even on his own turf, and his own religious upbringing didn't help the matter. Eunice certainly wanted Timothy to stay as far away as possible from the native Lycaonian religion, because it was morally corrupt. And Timothy's father wouldn't want the crudity and superstition of the native population to rub off on his son.

Timothy's separation from society was forced upon him. While separation has its advantages, it also has some built-in problems. For instance, how do you communicate with people from whom you are separated?

Perhaps this wasn't a problem for Timothy until he became a Christian. As a Jewish lad, he could be aloof and withdrawn from society, but as a Christian he was challenged to witness to his neighbors, whether they were Jews, Greeks, Romans, or Lycaonians. And all four groups were in Lystra. Timothy's foremost example was Paul, and Paul left no doubt that Christians should be bold in their witnessing.

But how?

You can drop a line with a hook on the end of it and a

worm daintily draped at the tip of the point, but that's not the way to *communicate* with fish.

You can hide yourself behind a duck blind and take a shot at an innocent bird up in the autumn sky, but that's not the way to *communicate* with ducks.

The expression "fishers of men" is used too loosely, and gives the wrong idea of what witnessing is all about. When God wanted to communicate with man, the Word became Flesh and dwelt among us, and yet was without sin. The secret ingredient of the most effective witnessing is not good bait, but divine love.

No doubt Timothy knew the Old Testament Scriptures, thanks to his mother, but it is doubtful that he knew much about people and how to talk with them until he rubbed shoulders with Paul. And Paul, who tried to become all things to all men that he might win some, was an exciting model for Timothy to copy. (See 1 Cor. 9:22.)

So while the Lystran mob wanted to offer sacrifices to Paul, Timothy was waiting to see how Paul would get out of this jam and turn the hubbub into an opportunity to communicate the Gospel.

Paul's Message

When the crowd finally quieted down, Paul spoke simply and directly to them. It is the first occasion recorded in the New Testament that Paul, or any of the apostles for that matter, addressed a completely pagan audience.

Basically, Paul's message was positive, although he referred to the Lystrans' religious practices as "worthless things" or "emptiness." Paul never avoided mentioning the necessity of repentance in his preaching. But the bulk of his message was about God, the true God that the Lystrans, like the Athenians (Acts 17), didn't know anything about.

Paul didn't try to be profound, or to impress the Lystrans with his erudition. He didn't quote Old Testament Scripture. Nor did he, as he did later to the more cultured Athenians, quote Greek poets. He spoke about Almighty God and said that He lives, He creates, He cares, and He reveals.

Paul presented Jehovah as the God who created all things and who sends the rain so crops can grow. That was something the Lystrans could understand. According to William M. Ramsey, "Strong contrasts of climate between the long severe winter and the short but hot summer, a fertile soil dependent entirely on the chances of an uncertain rainfall, impressed on the minds of the inhabitants the insignificance of man and his dependence on the power of nature" (*Historical Geography of Asia Minor,* Cooper Square, p. 333).

Zeus was regarded as the god of rain and Hermes was the dispenser of food, so when Paul identified himself as the spokesman for the God who provided both rain and food, it was obvious he represented a superior Deity. If one God could do the work of two, He must be better.

Paul couldn't speak to the Lystrans in Jewish terms. He couldn't refer to Abraham, Isaac, and Jacob or tell his listeners that Jesus was the Son of David, and the long-promised Messiah. They wouldn't have understood what he was talking about.

Actually, what Paul said is somewhat similar to what he later told another totally pagan audience, the Athenians on Mars Hill.

First, Paul identified with his audience. "We are men of like passions as you are." Obviously, he wanted them to know that he wasn't a god and that they should stop that silly sacrifice business. But besides that, he was attempting to build a bridge between himself and his audience. The only other time in Scripture where this phrase is used is in the Epistle of James, where the Old Testament Prophet Elijah is described as a "man of like passions." Since first-century Jews had a penchant for making Elijah into a superhuman, James told his audience that Elijah had the same emotions and feelings they had. He was just a man too.

Next, Paul told the Lystrans what his business was. The word he used is literally "good newser." Paul and Barnabas were "good newsers."

Timothy knew very well that good news was a scarce commodity in Lystra. The city was past its prime, and the people were not prosperous. Lystra had more than its share of beggars, soldiers, and shepherds; but it had not seen many good newsers lately.

Lystrans who listened carefully to what Paul was saying—and granted, there probably weren't too many— would have noted that Paul's God was different indeed from their own. He showed concern for man, and that was a revolutionary idea. He was not a capricious, game-playing god who toyed with creation, nor an absentee god, off on an extended vacation. Paul's God was involved with man's daily physical needs, but more than that, He was concerned with man's moral and spiritual needs.

What Paul did here might be termed pre-evangelism, loosening the soil so that a Timothy, or a Eunice, or another new convert could plant a seed on fertile ground. Later Paul told the Corinthians, "I have planted, Apollos watered, but God gave the increase" (1 Cor. 3:6). In Lystra, however, Paul was taking a preliminary step.

A Lystran who had heard Paul speak at this time might have asked: "You say that your God is concerned; how has He shown His concern? You say that God reveals Himself to man. Has your God ever come down like Zeus and Hermes to dwell among men?" And then it would have been up to Timothy or some other Christian to begin to share the whole counsel of God.

At times we feel that we must give the complete Gospel story at every opportunity, as if we didn't believe that the Holy Spirit is big enough to take control of the situation. By cramming too much food down his throat, we might be giving the witnessee spiritual indigestion. We must be faithful in our witness and take each opportunity that presents itself, but we need not feel guilt-ridden if God only opens the door a crack.

Despite Paul's protests, the crowd was not easily convinced that Paul and Barnabas weren't Greek gods. The language barrier may have been a problem. But eventually, the tumult died, and the festivities to honor the visiting "deities" were halted.

For Paul, it must have been a frustrating day, like a ball game rained out after four innings of play when you are ahead twelve to nothing. The day had started out so well with a miracle, but it had ended with confusion. Half of the crowd hadn't understood him and the other half hadn't seemed to believe him.

That's the way it must have seemed to Paul. But for teenaged Timothy, the event must have been incredibly exciting—an unbelievable day in the life of a new Christian. And the excitement wasn't over yet.

Today we speak of hero worship and of teenage idols. Even in Christian circles, celebrities are placed on pedestals, like busts of Greek gods. Newly converted entertainers and athletes are heralded, as if they had descended from the skies. People listen to their utterances as if the nectar of the gods were constantly dropping from their lips.

At that moment in Lystra, Paul was Timothy's idol. If Paul had permitted the crowd's adulation to continue, it would have been perilous, not only to himself but also to young Timothy. Paul was a leader, but not a god. He could be followed, but not worshiped. His words had to be regarded, but he was not to be revered. When he spoke, he spoke not of himself, except to identify himself as the good newser of the great God. Any time a person is lifted up, he must be careful lest he obscure the Son, the One who declared, "And I, if I be lifted up from the earth, will draw all men unto Me" (John 12:32).

More Visitors to Lystra

Not long afterward, other visitors came to the isolated outpost of Lystra. Perhaps they had heard of the excitement there. Or they may have heard descriptions of Paul and Barnabas and recognized them as the men who had been driven out of Antioch and Iconium a few weeks earlier. If the Lystrans had any lingering doubt about the identities of the two itinerant rabbis, these new visitors could set the record straight.

TV westerns show con men going from town to town, fleecing the citizens of all they can get and then quickly moving on to another town for riper pickings. That's how these latest visitors portrayed Paul and Barnabas. Before long, the fickle crowd was chanting for the blood of the two missionaries.

Talk about having ups and downs! They were worshiped as gods one day and accused of being con men the next.

What would be fitting punishment for these two who had so treacherously fooled the people?

The visiting vigilantes would have mentioned that the Jewish punishment of stoning had been authorized by the Romans for Jews who had desecrated the temple; Paul and Barnabas had almost desecrated the temple of Zeus in front of Lystra. Then the uproar began anew.

Stones began to rain on Paul. As they fell on him, he must have thought of Stephen, the first Christian martyr. Paul had been in hearty agreement with that stoning. And he had been close enough to hear Stephen pray, "Lord, do not hold this sin against them." (See Acts 7:60.) Now Paul was the one falling beneath a volley of stones.

As the Lystrans heaved rocks at him, perhaps he recognized the faces of some who had been ready to deify him only a short time before. He might have recalled how the Lord Himself had been brought into Jerusalem with the shouts of "Hosanna" one day and taunted out of town with the cries of "Crucify Him, Crucify Him," only a few days later. "The servant," Jesus had said, "is not above his master." (See John 13:16.) Now Paul was the one facing death at the hands of a fickle mob.

Timothy—impressionable Timothy—must have been nearby. He hadn't known Paul long, but during that time he certainly had developed a deep attachment for this man who was 30 years his senior.

Never in Timothy's life had so much happened in such a short time. Like teenagers through the ages in all parts of the world, he had probably complained, "Nothing ever happens around here."

No doubt he had good reason for his complaint. Lystra was certainly not the most exciting town for a 16-year-old.

But with Paul and Barnabas came excitement, lots of it. They made things happen. Not only had Timothy become a Christian, but he had begun following Paul around, listening, watching, observing—soaking up knowledge of his newfound faith.

Then came that exciting day when the cripple was healed and the crowd wanted to make sacrifices to Paul and Barnabas. Talk about excitement!

And then the stoning. Paul, the man who had brought Timothy spiritual life, lay motionless on a rubble heap outside the city, where men had dragged him. Life and death came so close together.

Was this what being a Christian was all about? Would this lie ahead for Timothy too, if he followed Paul's example?

Great Expectations

Christianity often stirs great expectations—some of them false.

What do you expect from Christianity? Is Jesus Christ a magic elixir? Will the rest of your life be trouble-free?

If Timothy had wondered about such questions, he found some hard answers as he saw Paul bombarded by rocks.

If his mother Eunice had any doubts about her son leading a life of security and enjoyment as a disciple of Jesus Christ, she too was jarred into reality that day.

I'm impressed with the courage of that small band of new Christians who gathered around the battered apostle. According to early church tradition, Timothy was one of them. The angry mob that had just finished stoning Paul could easily have turned against this little group of Christians.

What about these new converts in Lystra? Wouldn't it have been a prudent time to reassess their commitments? After all, they would have to live with neighbors in the community for the rest of their lives. It would have been easy at this point to step back into the old way of life. But Timothy didn't think that way. He may have been frail and even timid, but he was faithful. He could always be counted on to be at the right place at the right time. And at this time, the right place was beside Paul.

What a surprise the new converts had! Suddenly, from

amid the rubble, the seemingly lifeless form began to stir. The eyelids flickered, the muscles twitched. Paul was alive. "As the disciples stood round about him, he rose up, and came into the city" (Acts 14:20).

Tradition says that he stayed that night in the home of Eunice and Lois, the mother and grandmother of Timothy.

Years later, in Paul's final epistle to Timothy, he reminded his "son in the faith" that "all who desire to live godly in Christ Jesus will be persecuted." And he referred to persecutions and sufferings, "such as happened to me at Antioch, at Iconium and at Lystra; what persecutions I endured, *and out of them all the Lord delivered me!*" (2 Tim. 3:11-12, NASB) Did God deliver him at Lystra?

The great commentator G. Campbell Morgan wrote, From Antioch Paul was allowed to escape and was preserved. At Iconium God overruled circumstances; he was warned and escaped. But he did not escape from Lystra. We cannot say that God took care of him at Antioch and at Iconium and that He did not take care of him at Lystra. . . . At Antioch and Iconium, He delivered him by saving him from the stones. At Lystra, He delivered him through stoning. . . . Sometimes the only deliverance God can work for us is by the way of the stones, and by furnace experiences (*The Acts of the Apostles,* Revell, p. 344).

The Missionaries Move On

Farewells are seldom easy, but for Timothy, saying good-bye to Paul must have been especially difficult. Would he ever see this fearless man again?

Paul had come into Lystra recovering from an illness; he left one day after having been stoned and dumped unceremoniously outside the city. To Timothy, Paul must have seemed an intrepid warrior who would never succumb to physical complaints.

Think of Timothy as he watched Paul, perhaps assisted by Barnabas, limping out of the city gates, down the Imperial Highway, and disappearing out of sight on his way to the next town of Derbe, 60 miles southeast.

Paul no doubt had said that he planned to come back to Lystra as soon as he could. But how soon would that be, if ever? With Paul's penchant for stirring up riots, he might never get past Derbe.

It didn't make sense for Paul to return to Lystra in the near future. For one thing, the Lystrans had just stoned him. For another thing, Derbe was on the way to Paul's home base of Antioch in Syria, and halfway between Derbe and Antioch was Paul's hometown of Tarsus. So it would have been tempting for Paul to keep on going eastward to Antioch.

Paul, however, didn't take the shortest way home. It may have been the weather; winter snow often closed the Cilician Gates in the Taurus Mountains through which Paul would have had to go en route to Tarsus. Also, Paul carried a deep concern for his fledgling churches. He wanted to make sure that persecution hadn't dampened the enthusiasm of the young converts.

So after a fruitful ministry in Derbe, Paul retraced his steps through Lystra, Iconium, and Pisidian Antioch, encouraging believers, warning them that more persecution lay ahead, and organizing them into structured fellowships. Church leaders who had been chosen by the people were confirmed and appointed by Paul.

This time Paul's visit didn't make headlines. Perhaps it was because his ministry was directed primarily toward the young churches. Or maybe the Roman leadership of the cities had changed while Paul was ministering in Derbe. Regardless, Timothy must have been both delighted and impressed to see this man courageously return to Lystra after having been stoned only a few months earlier.

When Paul told the small flock of believers in Lystra that it was through many tribulations that they would enter the kingdom of God (Acts 14:22), it was obvious to Timothy that Paul knew from personal experience what he was talking about.

No teenager likes to look forward to a life of tribulation. Yet this was the forecast that Paul had for Timothy: "It may be sunny today but there may be storm clouds tomorrow." A Christian leader who gives any other forecast does not know his Bible.

For Timothy it meant facing challenges that seemed too big for him. This would be enough to give anyone a Timothy complex.

• "Why doesn't God cut the problems down to my size?

• "Doesn't He know I'm no spiritual giant?

• "What's the sense of becoming a Christian if it simply ushers me into a lifetime of testing?"

Good questions. What's the sense of wanting to become pure gold if you have to go through the refiner's fire?

Yes, Paul left Timothy with a lot to think about. Another young man, Mark, hadn't liked big problems and had turned back.

Would Timothy also turn back?

3

The Fickle and the Faithful

It always happens. Just after you make a decision for Christ, the roof caves in. Usually it isn't a literal roof; often it's something more basic than plaster and tile.

The problem is that there's often no one around to give help. You're all alone.

You may be in a difficult time at work. If your pastor were there, probably he could keep you cool and guide you through the situation. But he isn't there. You have to face it alone.

Timothy had a similar experience shortly after he became a Christian. His spiritual father Paul was on his way back to Antioch of Syria, nearly 300 miles away. The new churches in Pisidian Antioch, Iconium, Lystra, and Derbe had just been organized. Their new leaders were inexperienced. They were new Christians who were still trying to understand all that the Apostle Paul had been telling them. And at the same time they had the responsibility to teach those truths to others.

The churches were growing too. Most of the new growth seemed to be among the Gentile population. Ir

Lystra, Timothy must have watched this church expansion with amazement. Even without Paul and Barnabas on the scene, new converts were being added regularly.

Then a third set of visitors came to Lystra. (It was a good year for Lystra's motel business.) The first visitors, of course, were Paul and Barnabas, who came to preach the Gospel. The second visitors were Jews, upset by the way the new teaching was dividing their synagogues in Iconium and Antioch of Pisidia. They were the ones who saw to it that Paul was stoned.

The third group of visitors seem to have been Jewish converts to Christianity, though not all scholars agree to that. It's even possible that some of the same people in the second group were now returning with this third group. Their philosophy may have been: "If you can't fight 'em, join 'em, and then you can fight 'em from the inside."

Regardless of who they were, it was what they taught that was significant and also devastating to the young churches.

Here's the way this third group of visitors might have approached the young Christians in the church at Lystra:

VISITORS: The Scriptures teach that you must be circumcised if you want to be considered as God's people.

CHURCH: Paul said that is just for Jewish people, and that Gentile Christians don't need to be circumcised.

VISITORS: But how can you claim to believe the Scriptures and yet refuse to accept circumcision? And what about keeping the Sabbath and remembering the Passover and things like that?

CHURCH: Are those things really necessary?

VISITORS: Of course, they are. They're in the Scriptures aren't they? I think we better have a Bible study here and acquaint you folks with the Laws of Moses.

Confusion

Widespread confusion! John Drane, in his book, *Paul: An Illustrated Documentary* writes: "But when these new Christians began to read the Old Testament under the guidance of these Jewish Christians, they found themselves faced with a mass of rules and regulations which they knew they could never hope to fulfill, even if it was necessary to do so for salvation. Some of them decided to make a brave attempt, and began by keeping the Jewish Sabbath and possibly certain other Jewish festivals as well. A large number of them began to think about being circumcised, in order to fulfill what seemed to be the requirements of the Old Testament. But the great majority simply did not know what to do" (Harper and Row, p. 47).

Probably Timothy didn't know what to do either. As a Jewish boy who hadn't been circumcised (no doubt because his father had opposed the practice), he was caught in the middle. He could easily have succumbed to the teaching of these Jewish leaders. But one thing must have bothered him—what people were saying about Paul. They were implying that Paul didn't know what he was talking about. And worse.

The conversation might have gone something like this:

VISITORS: Whom did you say taught you this strange idea—that all you have to do is believe in Jesus and you will be saved?

CHURCH: Paul did.

VISITORS: Paul who?

CHURCH: Paul of Tarsus.

VISITORS: Paul of Tarsus?

CHURCH: He's a missionary from the church of Antioch in Syria.

VISITORS: Antioch in Syria? Don't you think it would have been better for you to learn from the mother church in Jerusalem? You know, in Jerusalem there are apostles, men whom Jesus actually commissioned and told to become missionaries. Peter, James, John, and Andrew are there, and Paul isn't one of them, you know.

CHURCH: But don't they teach the same thing Paul teaches?

VISITORS: Well, Paul is supposed to teach the same things they teach. But the trouble is, he doesn't. He's all mixed up now.

CHURCH: We think Paul has been in Jerusalem talking to those apostles.

VISITORS: Sure, and probably they allowed him to preach, but they didn't authorize him to say what he's saying.

CHURCH: What do you mean?

VISITORS: You've never been to Jerusalem, have you?

CHURCH: No, we haven't.

VISITORS: Some of us have, and we've talked to Peter, James, and John. And do you know what?

CHURCH: What?

VISITORS: Every one of those apostles is circumcised; every one of them keeps the Law of Moses. And if you want to be a full-fledged member of the church, you'd better do the same.

CHURCH: But Paul said . . .

VISITORS: Is Paul an apostle?

CHURCH: He sure sounded like one.

VISITORS: Well, he isn't. And the only authority he has comes from the real apostles in Jerusalem. But there's still hope for you. If you stay with us, we can straighten out your errors.

If Timothy ever got involved in a conversation like that, it is easy to imagine his reaction. It must have hurt him to see many others whom he knew—both Jews and Gentiles—buying the line of the new teachers and attacking Paul as teaching a half-truth or even purposely distorting the Gospel of the apostles.

But there was another line of argument against Paul's message that might have gone something like this:

VISITORS: By the way, what was the first thing that attracted you to the way of the Scriptures?

CHURCH: The lives of the people. Immorality is so rampant these days. It's awful to see the way people carry on in public: prostitution, drunkenness, crime in the streets, and no shame about it, either. The only place we don't see this going on is within the Jewish community.

VISITORS: And you know why you don't see it in the Jewish community?

CHURCH: Why?

VISITORS: Because of the Laws of Moses. Take away the Laws of Moses, and the Jews will become just as depraved as everyone else. And that's the trouble with what your friend Paul is teaching.

CHURCH: What do you mean?

VISITORS: He says Gentile converts are free from the Law. Freedom—that's the word he uses a lot.

CHURCH: That's right; he does. He often refers to Christian freedom. He says it's important.

VISITORS: Freedom is a dangerous word. If new converts follow the way of freedom as Paul teaches it, pretty soon your church will be no different from the pagan temples. You'll have orgies and drunken riots instead of worship of Jehovah.

CHURCH: We hadn't thought of that.

VISITORS: Well, probably Paul didn't think of that either. We're afraid he didn't think through what he was saying in a lot of areas. You know, even if there were some truth in what he was saying, it wouldn't be worth the risk.

The visitors had claimed to be Christians; they had even claimed to be strengthening Paul's teaching by adding to it. But when they had finished, there wasn't much left of authentic Christianity. They had claimed to be a "truth squad," following hard on Paul's heels, with more of the same Gospel. But it wasn't more of the same. It was something totally different.

Three Basics

They challenged three basic ideas of Christianity: salvation, sanctification, and authority. They questioned (1) how to become a Christian; (2) how to successfully live a Christian life; and (3) how to know what to believe and do.

These three basic ideas are repeatedly challenged today. While some other ideas can be held more loosely, these three need to be held as firmly as possible.

My guess is that Timothy may have gotten confused upon the arrival of this latest group of visitors, but I doubt if he ever lost his footing on these basic planks of Christianity. If he had, I think that Paul, when he wrote those two epistles to Timothy later in life, would have mentioned Timothy's tendency to waver.

Paul and Peter in Antioch

It wasn't long before Paul got wind of the fact that there was trouble in Galatia, or more technically, the southern part of the Roman province of Galatia. Paul had nearly lost his life two or three times in the founding of these churches; according to the reports he was receiving, they were defecting. He had worked so hard, and now his work seemed to be evaporating.

At the time, Paul seemed surrounded by problems. After his exhausting missionary journey—illness, stoning, howling mobs, etc.,—he should have been entitled to a quiet missionary furlough. But he certainly wasn't going to get a quiet furlough in Antioch of Syria.

First of all, about the time that Paul got back to Antioch, Simon Peter came to visit. (Scholars are not sure whether Peter's visit occurred before or after Paul's first missionary journey, but many, such as Merrill Tenney, F.F. Bruce, Alan Cole, and William Ramsey, date it at this point.) Peter may have wanted to get a firsthand report on the missionary journey of Paul and Barnabas, or he may simply have wanted to see how the church in Antioch was progressing.

At any rate, it was a pleasant visit, at least for a while. Peter was mixing easily with both the Jews and the Gentiles who composed the church in Antioch. He participated in the love feasts without regard to the backgrounds of the Christians involved.

Then, some visitors once again spelled trouble (Gal. 2:12; Acts 15:1). These came from Jerusalem and seemed to be shocked by the way Jewish Christians—even Simon Peter—mingled with Gentile Christians as if there were no difference. And they were rigid in declaring: "Unless you are circumcised according to the custom of Moses, you cannot be saved" (Acts 15:1, NASB).

Naturally, Paul was riled. But what angered Paul more was that Peter himself stopped eating with the Gentiles; and not only Peter but also Barnabas. As F.F. Bruce puts it, "The last man of whom it might have been expected—was persuaded to join in withdrawing from table fellowship with Gentiles" (*Apostle of the Heart Set Free,* Eerdmans, p. 177).

Paul saw the implication immediately. If this continued, it meant that there could be no unity in God's family. The Gentiles would always be second-class citizens until they became circumcised. And if they consented to become circumcised, it meant that their salvation would be by faith plus circumcision and not by faith alone.

Paul couldn't allow Peter's action to go unchallenged. He was well aware of Peter's position in the church at Jerusalem. Yet he felt he had to rebuke Peter publicly for the sake of the future of the Gospel.

Now any time two dominant leaders of a church are at odds, the atmosphere is tinged with emotion. The church at Antioch was no exception during those days. Paul later wrote to the Romans, "As much as lieth in you, live peaceably with all men" (Rom. 12:18). But this was one time when Paul felt it wasn't possible. The cause of the Gospel was at stake. Peter had to be rebuked.

About that time, Paul received word of the same kind of trouble in the Galatian churches, the churches for which he had risked his life.

Probably he would have liked to pack up and get to Galatia as quickly as possible to straighten things out. Obviously, he couldn't.

He had to stay in Antioch to keep that church from drifting back into Judaism. If "even Barnabas" was swayed by the visitors from Jerusalem, the church of Antioch couldn't afford to send Paul even on a short visit to Galatia.

A Letter to the Galatians

Yet he needed to respond quickly to those churches. Every day he delayed might mean another soul deluded by the Judaizers. So in the middle of the maelstrom of confusion, frustration, and concern, Paul sat down to write a letter to the new churches in Galatia.

Even as he wrote the letter, he must have realized that he would have to have a summit conference with the apostolic leaders in Jerusalem to get the problems ironed out, once and for all. But the problems in Galatia had to be confronted immediately. He couldn't wait for some future conference to act.

It was the first of 12 or more letters that Paul was to write in the next 20 years. And perhaps it was the most emotional. Someone has termed it the "explosive epistle." In places, it snaps, crackles, and pops. It was addressed to a group of churches, rather than to a single church. It would have been sent as a circular letter to be read in each Galatian church, perhaps following the same course that Paul himself had originally taken: first, the church in Pisidian Antioch, then the church in Iconium, then the church in Timothy's town of Lystra, and finally the youngest church in Derbe.

All sorts of rumors had been circulating about Paul. By the time the letter arrived, most of the Galatians may have been so confused that they didn't know what to believe about him. Perhaps they felt like asking, "Will the real Paul of Tarsus please stand up?"

Was Paul wishy-washy? Was he merely a man-pleaser? Did he soften the demands of the Old Testament? Was he making up his theology as he went along? Did he have any authority to teach as he did? Who was Paul anyway?

Rumors and Faith

Suppose you heard a rumor at the office that the boss was going to give everyone a $100 bonus at the end of the month.

If your reaction were the same as mine, you'd ask: "Who says?"

The answer to that question would determine how much credence you would attach to the rumor. Look at some of these possible replies and evaluate whether they would help you to credit or discredit the rumor.

• "I heard it in the cafeteria line. I'm not quite sure who said it, but the man sounded as if he knew what he was talking about.''

• ''Well, that's what Ethel told me, and you know her best friend is Maude who is the sister of the sales manager, and he has an appointment with the big boss every week.''

• ''I read it on the bulletin board downstairs. The notice wasn't signed and I thought that was a bit unusual, but the typing looked as if it had come from the boss' secretary. Most of the words were spelled correctly.''

• ''I just had a meeting with the big boss himself, and he said that he would be making an official announcement this afternoon.''

It's interesting to analyze why a person tends to believe what he does. Let me mention three things that influence trust or belief.

1. The extent of your belief in a statement is in direct proportion to the extent of your trust in the person who made the statement to you. Obviously, if the office practical joker had told you about the end-of-the-month bonus, it would be extremely hard to believe him, even if for once he was telling the truth.

2. Belief comes easiest when it is compatible with past beliefs. In other words, if the boss had given out end-of-the-month bonuses before, it would be much easier to believe that he would do it again. If he was known to be a tightwad, who would believe the story until the $100 check was cashed?

3. It is always hard to believe that a person will give you something for nothing. We're tempted to say, ''What's the catch? How much overtime does he expect next week? Does this mean no vacation next summer? There's got to be a catch somewhere.''

Now translate all of that into the problem that the Galatians faced in the first century.

A man named Paul had come to town saying that salvation came by the grace of God through faith and faith alone. Salvation didn't depend on circumcision or on keeping the Ten Commandments. It depended on what Christ had already done on the Cross.

Shortly after Paul left, the Judaizers came to town saying, "Paul was wrong. Sure, you need to believe in Jesus, but you also need to be circumcised. Paul didn't know what he was talking about."

Whom should the Galatians believe?

Well, it might depend on the extent of their trust in the person who made the statement. It might also depend on what seemed the most compatible with past beliefs. Or it might depend on whether they could believe that God would give them everything for nothing.

There were psychological roadblocks which had to be dealt with and disposed of, if the young church was to grow.

Was Paul a person who could be trusted? Did he really know what he was talking about?

When it comes to receiving a bonus, the person to trust is the one closest to the boss. And the Judaizers were saying that Paul came from Antioch, not from Jerusalem where the apostles resided.

In fact, the Judaizers implied that they had received their message from Jerusalem, from the apostles themselves. And when they said *apostles,* you can be sure they emphasized *apostles* as if Paul were only a pseudo-apostle. If Paul got any instructions from the apostles at all, he had certainly gotten them all garbled by now, they implied.

Well, Paul had his work cut out for him.

Imagine the excitement in Lystra when his letter arrived. Try to guess how Timothy felt as he sat in the small congregation listening to the Epistle to the Galatians being read for the first time. Running through his mind may have been questions such as: *Does Paul really know what he's talking about? What right has he to say what he is saying? Is salvation really as easy as he says? If so, won't it encourage people to sin? Will he really tackle the issues head-on or will he try to sidestep them?*

Paul's Defense

As soon as one of the elders began to read the letter to the congregation, they knew for certain that Paul was tackling the issues head-on.

The words were forceful and electric: "Paul, an apostle (not of men, neither by man, but by Jesus Christ, and God the Father, who raised Him from the dead)" (Gal. 1:1).

There was no doubt about it. This was the real Paul standing up. He wasted no time in identifying himself as an apostle and in declaring that his message had come directly from God (vv. 11-12).

In most of Paul's other epistles, he included a word of thanks or commendation at the beginning, immediately after his salutation. That was the polite way to write a letter in those days. Paul even found something for which he could praise God in the problem-ridden church of Corinth. But there is no such section in the letter to the Galatian churches. This was probably not because he couldn't have found anything praiseworthy to say. Rather, it was because he was writing so emotionally. He couldn't stand on formality. He had to plunge immediately into the problem.

So he did. "I am astonished," he wrote, "that you are so quickly deserting the One who called you" (1:6, NIV). Paul said that they moved away from the truth of the Gospel. "I don't care who told you to move," Paul went on to say. "Even if I told you, or even for that matter if an angel told you, it is an accursed idea and the preachers of that message should be accursed too." (See Gal. 1:8-9.)

Blunt language. When Paul referred to an angel from heaven, he may have been thinking back to his first visit to Lystra and how the local townsfolk had thought that he and Barnabas had dropped in out of the sky like angels.

It was obvious that Paul was upset, and for good reason. The Galatians weren't playing around with different versions of the evening news. They were playing with fire, hellfire. Of course, Paul was excited.

It is hard to read the Letter to the Galatians in a monotone. No matter who read it in the Galatian churches, it must have been a moving experience to hear it for the first time as Timothy did.

The first two chapters of Galatians contain Paul's thumbnail biography. He wrote how, prior to his conversion, he had been a zealous Pharisee, climbing the ladder of success in his profession by being a bounty hunter of Christians. With that background, who would think it likely he would say that circumcision and keeping of the Law were irrelevant to salvation?

He told of his conversion on the Damascus Road, emphasizing the divine aspect of it. God had "set him apart"; God had "called him"; God had "revealed His Son" to him. His salvation was not something that he had merited; it was all through the grace of God. (See 1:15-16.)

Anyone paying attention at all—and what Lystran wasn't?—would have gotten the point. Paul couldn't have dreamed up his message on his own; nor would he have watered down the Jewish aspects of the Gospel to make it more palatable to the Gentiles. He was only doing what God had told him to do. He was conveying to the Galatians the message that God had given him.

In other words, Paul said, "If you don't like the Gospel that I'm preaching, don't blame me; blame God. It was all God's doing."

Paul realized that if his salvation depended on himself, he would still be hunting down Christians. But God had called him and he had no doubts that the initiative belonged to God.

Similarly the message that He was preaching was God's message, not his own, and that gave him a boldness in preaching. You see, if you are called of God to go somewhere, and if God gives you the message to preach, you don't have to worry; you are in God's hands, and there is no safer place to be.

Those were lessons that young Timothy would still have to learn. He was worried about his own inadequacy to cope with bigger-than-life situations.

But if it is God who has taken the initiative to save you and to give you a message, then you do not need to worry about your own inadequacy. If the vertical relationship is sure, it doesn't matter how unknown the horizontal relationships may be.

In the latter half of Galatians 1, Paul emphasized that his authority came vertically, not horizontally. He did not consult with other apostles about what he should preach. It was more important to consider God's sovereignty before thinking of man's response. And it was important to consider communion with God before taking time for fellowship with the brethren. Lonely Arabia had to come before busy Jerusalem.

There's no denying that Paul's life was a busy one, just as Christ's life had been. But just as Jesus had felt it necessary to go out to pray "a great while before day," so Paul had felt it essential to go to Arabia for 3 years before entering 30 years of Christian ministry.

In our day, fellowship has become more popular than

worship. Sometimes our commitments for communion with man make it difficult for us to have time for communion with God. Even if the fellowship is Christian fellowship and the business is Christian service, we have our priorities mixed up and need to find our way back to Arabia.

When Paul did arrive in Jerusalem three years later, the disciples were afraid of him (Acts 9:26), until Barnabas took him under his wing. It seems that even with Barnabas at Paul's side, only James, the Lord's brother, and Peter spent any time with him.

For 12 to 14 years afterward (the Jews measured time a little differently from the way we do; parts of a year were counted as whole years), Paul was preaching and teaching the Gospel in Antioch of Syria and Tarsus in Cilicia. Then he visited Jerusalem again. This visit (Gal. 2) is probably the same one Luke mentioned (Acts 11:30), although scholars are by no means in agreement on this. Although the primary purpose of this visit was to bring funds for famine relief to the poverty-stricken Christians in and around Jerusalem, Paul took the opportunity to spell out in detail his theological approach to the Gentiles. He wanted to make sure that his preaching was in line with the teaching of the other apostles. After the meeting, the other apostles shook hands with Barnabas and Paul and encouraged them to continue preaching the Gospel to the Gentiles.

All of this Paul spelled out in his letter (Gal. 1—2).

By this time Paul had made his major points: (1) His message had come from God, not man; (2) it was not the kind of a message that he from his Pharisaic background would have dreamed up on his own; and (3) the apostles were in full agreement with his message.

Agreement, yes.

But not always understanding all its implications.

As F.F. Bruce states: "Paul's position was clear-cut because he had thought it through; the Jerusalem leaders had not yet had any occasion to think it through" (*Apostle of the Heart,* p. 181).

So Paul assisted them in the thought process. He described one example (Gal. 2) which I have mentioned earlier. Peter had come to Antioch and while he was there he had equal fellowship in every way with both Jews and Gentiles. Soon other Jews from Jerusalem arrived; then as one version puts it, Peter began "to hold himself aloof." So Paul had to help Peter "think it through."

The conversation between Peter and Paul might have gone something like this:

PAUL: Didn't you tell me that Jesus said He came to call sinners, not the righteous, to repentance, that He came to find the lost sheep and call the prodigal back home?

PETER: Yes, that's right.

PAUL: And didn't you tell me that on the Day of Pentecost you preached and told the crowd that all they needed to do was repent and believe?

PETER: Yes, that's right.

PAUL: Was it the Law that brought salvation to these people?

PETER: No, of course not. It was Jesus.

PAUL: What did the Law do for them then?

PETER: All it did was to show us that we are sinners and that we need a Saviour.

PAUL: And by admitting that you're a sinner, aren't you putting yourself on the same basis as the Gentiles, as far as salvation is concerned?

PETER: That's right. I realized this when I baptized Cornelius the centurion.

PAUL: So there is no difference between Jew and Gentile, as far as salvation is concerned?

PETER: Right. Salvation has nothing to do with keeping the Law. It comes by faith in Jesus Christ alone.

PAUL: Then why did you stop eating with the Gentiles when your friends from Jerusalem came? Why are those rules and regulations so important to you?

PETER: Well, they aren't important for salvation, but I didn't want to lead those Jerusalem brethren into sin.

PAUL: But if by eating with Gentiles you were showing your Christian oneness with them, then Jesus must have been leading you into sin.

PETER: Jesus wouldn't lead anyone into sin.

PAUL: I know that. So don't you see how absurd your position is?

PETER: Well, I can see that it is not very consistent, but then consistency has never been my strongest feature. Tell me, Paul, if you don't have rules and regulations to follow, how do you live a holy life?

PAUL: Well, Peter, every day I see myself as crucified with Christ. So in a sense, the old Paul is dead. And yet, of course, I am still alive. But the new life I have, I am living by faith in the One who loved me and gave Himself for me. If the cross of Christ was big enough to save me, it is also big enough to keep me. (See Gal. 2:20.)

Paul wasn't interested in telling the Galatians that he had put Peter in his place. But he was interested in establishing his credibility. Could the Galatians trust him? Did he know what he was talking about? Was he really an apostle as he said he was? Was he trustworthy in matters of eternal significance?

Of course, Paul's real purpose in establishing his credibility concerned the nature of the Gospel itself. Could the Galatians trust Paul regarding salvation? The question was not a legal one, like whether they could prepare a meal on the Sabbath. It was: "How are you saved?" It was the real core of Christianity.

And the gist of Paul's argument is found in the question: "Did you receive the Spirit by observing the Law or by believing what you heard?" (Gal. 3:2, NIV)

There was no question about the answer, but Paul asked the same question in a different way: "When God does miracles, is this by faith or by the Ten Commandments?"

Once again there was no question about the answer.

So Paul hammered his point home. "How was Abraham saved? Abraham believed God and it was counted to him as righteousness." (See Gen. 15:6.) That was before God gave the rite of circumcision.

"But," Paul argued, "suppose a person wants to be saved by the Law anyway. Well, the Law requires perfection. If a man isn't 100 percent perfect, he is under its curse." And Paul was sure there weren't many 100 percent perfect people walking around Galatia (Gal. 3:10-12).

Paul had made his point. All the way through the Epistle to the Galatians, there is strong language, and yet there is a tenderness also (see Gal. 4:12-20, for example). He spoke as a concerned father might address a wayward child.

It was obvious that Paul was disappointed in the Galatians. They were easily movable and fickle. Some scholars feel that this was a national trait; whether this is true or not, these Galatians certainly demonstrated their instability at this point.

While the Galatians did not seem to possess the quality of steadfastness, Timothy did. He had other weaknesses and frailties, but he was reliable; he was trustworthy; and he was faithful.

It is difficult to be faithful when everyone around is wavering. It is difficult to be faithful when you know how weak and timid you are. But the thing that impressed Paul about Timothy was his faithfulness (1 Cor. 4:17).

In Galatians 5, Paul outlined the fruit of the Spirit and mentioned the word *faith* as seventh on the list. Many modern versions translate the word as *faithfulness*; Barclay says "that the best translation of all is simply *loyalty*." That was a fruit of the Spirit that Timothy possessed.

Jesus said, "He who is faithful in little things will also be faithful in much (see Luke 16:10). It was no little thing for Timothy to be faithful when others were denouncing Paul and following the teachings of the Judaizers.

But bigger tests for Timothy's faithfulness lay ahead of him.

Where Do We Go from Here?

Timothy, why would you want to join up with Paul? You're asking for trouble. How long have you known him—three years now, maybe four? And what's happened during those years?

Remember the first time you met him? He was soon stoned, dragged out of the city, and left for dead. Is that what you want to face in every town you visit?

Remember what happened immediately after Paul left? He was slandered, misrepresented, and misunderstood. In his letter he said that he was afraid that all his work had been in vain. Is that what you want out of life, Timothy? It may seem glamorous to visit foreign cities and unusual cultures, but if you make more enemies than friends, what good is it? What do you hope to accomplish?

And don't forget what kind of a person you are, Timothy. You're not a he-man type; you're Timothy, with close ties to your mother and grandmother. You're plunging in beyond your depth, Timothy. You'd be wiser to stay at home and become an elder in the church of Lystra. There's a lot of work to be done for God right here, you know.

Speaking of Eunice and Lois, don't you think you're needed here at home, Timothy? They're getting to an age when they will depend on you more than ever. You could be a merchant and do quite well in Lystra. If you want bigger things out of life, you might move 18 miles down the road to Iconium and establish yourself in business there.

No, Timothy, it just doesn't make sense to go with Paul to who-knows-where.

Advice to Paul

Paul, it doesn't make sense at all for you to choose Timothy as an aide. Do you remember the last time you did a thing like this? Barnabas brought along his nephew on your first missionary journey, and as soon as the going got rough, John Mark left you. Are you ready for that to happen again?

Not only that, Paul, but the conflict hurt a beautiful friendship between you and Barnabas. You decided that on this missionary journey, you wouldn't take a young man like Mark along with you. You'd take a seasoned veteran like Silas instead.

But you hardly get started on your trip and you ask young Timothy to join you; he's younger than Mark was. Paul, it just doesn't make sense.

And besides, look at Timothy. He isn't an Olympic athlete, you know. He'll probably have sore feet by the time he gets to Iconium. What help do you think he might be to you anyway? If he gets homesick, you'll have that to cope with too.

No, Paul, it seems like one of the more risky things you've ever done, and you've done some mighty risky things in your life.

A Message to Share

The year was A.D. 49. More than two years had passed since Paul's first missionary journey. He was close to 50 years old now; Timothy, nearly 19.

Those past two years had been eventful, to say the least. Not only had Paul headed off the Galatian heresy with his stern epistle, but after that he had traveled with Barnabas to Jerusalem (Acts 15) for a summit meeting with the leaders of the church at Jerusalem on the same problems. While accepting Paul's position, the Jerusalem leaders had asked that the new Gentile converts abstain from a few practices that were particularly offensive to Jews.

Furthermore, to settle any possible problems, they had put the whole thing in writing in an apostolic decree and had asked Paul to circulate it among the new churches.

It was probably with a great sense of relief that Paul and Barnabas headed back to Antioch again. The matter was finally settled for good; now they could get back to work.

When the church in Antioch heard the message from the church at Jerusalem, they rejoiced; unity was restored in the body of Christ. The whole church was at peace. The issue that had divided the church for several years had finally been settled.

Before long, Barnabas and Paul felt it was about time to share the good news with all the new churches they had established two or three years before. "Jerusalem and Antioch agree; Peter and Paul agree. There is only one Gospel. Jews and Gentiles are one in Jesus Christ; both find salvation in exactly the same way." (See Acts 15:23-29.)

But then a problem developed. It was such a small matter. Really.

Barnabas wanted to give his nephew Mark a second

chance. Kindhearted Barnabas, that's the way he was, always willing to take a risk on people. Years earlier, he had taken a risk with a new convert named Saul. The rest of the Christian church at Jerusalem had been scared out of their wits by the sound of Saul's name. But Barnabas was willing to take a risk that Saul was really a brother in Jesus Christ as he claimed to be. And you know the story from there.

Now Barnabas wanted to give Mark a second chance. Of course, Mark was a relative, so maybe the motives of Barnabas were tarnished a bit. Who knows?

But Paul was adamant: "This is a missionary journey, not a rehabilitation project. Mark had a chance, and he blew it. The stakes are too high for the success of this missionary expedition to be risked."

Christian vs. Christian

For centuries, people have argued whether Paul or Barnabas was wrong. If you want a third choice, maybe both were. And if you want a fourth, maybe neither was wrong.

At this point, nearly 2,000 years later, it matters little. But there are two things we can learn.

1. The devil doesn't like unity. At a time when the whole church was unified about the way of salvation, its two missionary leaders had a disagreement and had to part company. The two men who were just about to leave with the exciting message of oneness in Jesus Christ had to separate from each other because of a disagreement.

Just after you have completed the last stanza of "Blest Be the Tie That Binds," watch out.

2. God can accomplish His purposes anyway. The amazing thing is that God worked it out in true Romans 8:28 fashion for the good of all concerned. A disagreement between two Christian leaders isn't a good thing;

yet God can overrule.

Out of the disagreement came two missionary teams instead of one. Mark, the disappointment, was salvaged while working with his patient uncle and later became a valuable associate of the Apostle Paul (see Col. 4:10; Phile. 24; 2 Tim. 4:11). And, of course, if Mark had accompanied Paul on the second missionary journey, there would have been no need for Timothy to join Paul's troupe.

Paul's sidekick on the second journey was Silas, a member of the church of Jerusalem, and a strategic choice.

If there were any lingering questions among Galatian Christians about the necessity of following Old Testament practices, Paul could pull the official Jerusalem Decree out of his toga, signed and sealed by James, Peter, and the others. And he also had at his side a member of the Jerusalem church. "Even if you don't believe me," Paul could say, "you can believe Silas."

Silas may even have been the penman who wrote out the Jerusalem Decree, for its writing style bears a marked resemblance to the two Epistles to the Thessalonians which Silas wrote, as secretary to Paul.

Paul and Silas didn't follow the same route that Paul and Barnabas had taken on the first missionary journey. During that trip, Paul and Barnabas had gone to Cyprus first because that was Barnabas' native land. It seems that when Paul and Barnabas separated, they divided up the territory to be covered. Barnabas and Mark would go to Cyprus, which had been the locale of the first half of the first missionary journey, and Paul and Silas would go to Galatia, the locale of the second half.

So this time Paul probably went through his hometown of Tarsus, then across the Taurus Mountains by the Cilician Gates toward Derbe and Lystra, where the easternmost Galatian churches were located. At Lystra, Paul asked Timothy to join the tour.

But Why Timothy?

Let's probe Paul's possible reasons for choosing Timothy. In Scripture the most evident fact that is mentioned is that the Christians at Lystra and Iconium spoke well of Timothy. In a youth-oriented society as we have today, this may not seem remarkable. But in Paul's day when the elders were elder and no one under 30 was thought to be worth listening to, it was quite unusual.

It seems to me that there might have been several factors that led to Paul's invitation to Timothy.

1. Timothy got a good report card, not only from his home town of Lystra, but also from the neighboring town of Iconium, 18 miles away. In two or three years he had impressed the church leaders as an unusually faithful young man. He had remained true to the original message that Paul had preached.

2. A prophetic word confirmed Timothy as a good choice (1 Tim. 1:18). Silas was a prophet and it is quite possible that he was the one who pointed out Timothy.

3. No doubt Paul sensed a need that a young man like Timothy could meet. Timothy—part Jew, part Gentile—was a symbol of the blend of outreach that characterized Paul's ministry. Timothy knew the Old Testament from his mother's instruction and so he could assist in the instruction of new converts. Yet because he had grown up in a Gentile city, mingling with Gentiles wouldn't be as awkward for him as it might be for a Jerusalem Jew like Silas. Thirty years younger than Paul, Timothy represented a new generation of Christians. By adding him to the team, Paul would have representatives from three different churches: Jerusalem, Antioch, and Galatia. The more that Paul thought about it, the more sense it must

have made to him.

4. Paul might also have recognized Timothy's need to be challenged. If he stayed in Lystra, he could easily settle into a diffident life. Timothy needed to be transplanted into a bigger pot in order to develop deeper and stronger roots.

Certainly Paul recognized Timothy's limitations; undoubtedly, the unpleasant experience with John Mark was still fresh in Paul's mind. While adding another man to the team would multiply problems of interpersonal relations, the pluses outweighed the minuses; the pros outweighed the cons.

Thus, the invitation came to Timothy—a decision based on human considerations and supported by spiritual insight.

Not a bad way for any decision to be made.

Why Go with Paul?

What about Timothy? The decision wasn't only Paul's; it was Timothy's as well.

Many a church has extended a call to a pastor and then has been refused. Many people have applied for a job only to be turned down by a prospective employer. So both parties need to feel the same call.

What factors may have directed Timothy to join Paul and Silas? The Scriptures don't probe Timothy's mind on this matter, but probably we can surmise a few considerations that may have helped to influence him.

1. The encouragement of friends. My guess is that it was difficult for Timothy to know his own strengths and weaknesses. But the commendation of the Christian brethren at both Lystra and Iconium must have encouraged him.

2. The invitation of Paul himself. At times it may be necessary to make our own opportunities, but usually an open door prompts a decision. Timothy probably felt that God was offering him an open door to service.

3. The prophetic Word. No doubt the prophetic Word was as significant to Timothy as it was to Paul. The fact that Paul referred to this three times in his two letters to Timothy (written about 15 years later) is indicative of this.

4. The easiest or the best. For Timothy, the easiest thing to do would be to stay in Lystra with his mother and grandmother. But as he examined the need in his own life, it seemed to dovetail with Paul's need for an assistant with his qualifications.

But what about the uncertain future as a companion of Paul? What about possible suffering and deprivation? Timothy was probably convinced that such problems could be faced if he knew for certain that he was in the will of the Lord.

Preparation for a Mission Journey

Before Timothy left home, he was circumcised. This has raised a few questions, because Paul had written a lengthy and emotional letter to these same Galatians saying that circumcision was not necessary. In fact, he and Silas were at that very moment carrying letters from the Jerusalem council to the various churches saying the same thing. (See Acts 15:24.)

You might think that it didn't make sense for Paul to circumcise Timothy, until you remember that Timothy was a Jew. On this missionary journey he would be ministering in Jewish synagogues; if he were uncircumcised, his ministry would be greatly limited.

When Paul spoke of becoming all things to all men that he might win some, this is what he meant. He wasn't referring to twisting the Gospel or to watering it down to make it more palatable. He was speaking about not allowing anything to stand in the way of a forceful and effective presentation of the Gospel message.

I don't know what Paul told Timothy about the journey ahead, or about when he would see Eunice and Lois again. It would seem that Paul and Silas intended to travel in a clockwise circle (with Lystra being about 6 o'clock), and evangelize the whole of Asia Minor before returning with Timothy to Lystra again.

Maybe a little geography lesson here would be helpful. The continent of Asia today stretches from Japan, across China and India, and to the nation of Turkey. Sometimes Turkey is referred to as Asia Minor, and that's the area we will be considering in this chapter. This area, which is about 500 miles east to west and about 300 miles north to south, was composed in biblical times of several Roman provinces. These included Cilicia, Galatia, Bithynia, and to complicate matters more, Asia. Asia was the westernmost Roman province in Asia Minor, which in turn was the farthest west of the continent of Asia. So there were three Asias: (1) the province of Asia, the capital of which is Ephesus; (2) the area known as Asia Minor, which we know today as Turkey; and (3) the massive continent of Asia which extends from Japan to Turkey.

A Journey Begun

Paul's plan, as I said, was to evangelize the second area, known as Asia Minor. But nothing seemed to go according to plan.

Some people say that a person who follows God's leading will never be confused. But I think Paul, Silas, and Timothy were quite confused by the stops and starts in their travels.

Probably all went well in the first couple of cities. Paul had ministered in Iconium and Pisidian Antioch before and no doubt he revisited them first. Then came the confusion.

The troupe had gone from 6 o'clock to 7 o'clock on their clockwise circle. By veering off to their left, they could have ministered in such major cities as Ephesus, Colossae, Hierapolis, Laodicea, and Smyrna in the province of Asia. But apparently even before leaving Lystra, they received guidance from the Lord not to go in that direction. Paul's missionary philosophy was to tackle the big cities first, so it must have been puzzling to him that God did not want him to invade Ephesus with the Gospel.

As a young disciple, Timothy must have watched in awe as Paul and Silas determined the will of God as to where they were to minister. Paul always seemed to have a game plan, a strategy. He didn't let things happen helter-skelter. Yet coupled with his game plan was the awareness that his ways were not always God's ways. Paul had to be flexible and sensitive to the leading of the Holy Spirit.

While the Bible doesn't explicitly state what Paul's first game plan was, my guess is that it was to go as directly as possible to Ephesus, which may have had a population of nearly 500,000 people. Nearby were Smyrna and Pergamum each with populations close to 200,000. There were 500 cities in the province of Asia and some estimates put the population of the province at 4.6 million at the time. Little wonder that Paul wanted to go there.

But they "were forbidden of the Holy Ghost to preach the Word in Asia" (Acts 16:6). No explanation was given.

Nor is there any explanation as to how this message came to Paul. It is possible that once again it came through Silas the prophet.

Paul's second game plan was apparently to encompass the central land area of Asia Minor. But even this plan ran into some snags. After getting to 9 o'clock on their clockwise journey, the "Spirit suffered them not" to go to 10 o'clock (Acts 16:7).

As we read the Scriptures, these events flow into one another rather quickly and we see how God was directing them.

Frustration and Confusion

But as Paul and Silas and young Timothy were encountering this chain of frustrating and confusing events, the wisdom of God's plan wasn't so evident. They had walked nearly 250 miles, sometimes over mountainous terrain, not always sure where they were going, and being forbidden at crucial times to preach the Gospel.

Can you imagine the kind of letter that Timothy would have written home?

Dear Mom:

I'm not quite sure where we're going nor when we'll get back. We were going to Ephesus, but that didn't work out. Then we thought we should go to Bithynia but that didn't seem to work out either. Right now we are climbing over mountains in Mysia and fording mountain streams. I haven't seen anyone besides Paul and Silas for the last two days.

No, I haven't had a chance to do any preaching. For that matter, Paul hasn't either.

I'll write again if we ever get somewhere and if I can find out where we're going.

Love,
Tim

Such a letter is not very comforting to a mother. Yet that was the situation Timothy faced in his first few weeks with Paul and Silas. If Timothy had been like

John Mark, he would have turned around and gone home. If he had had a chance to preach, it wouldn't have been so bad. Timothy might even have preferred a little persecution for the sake of Jesus Christ, to wandering around uncertainly with his mouth closed. Was this what he had left Lystra to do?

Many Christians face the same kinds of uncertainties that Timothy did. Every way they turn, God seems to say, "Not yet," and they have no clear guidance as to what to do.

The best advice is to "hang in there," as Timothy did. Guidance will come. In the meantime, make your game plans, as Paul did. Keep moving. You may be heading for Ephesus when God says "No." You may not understand why God doesn't want you to evangelize one of the major cities in the world. But don't sit on your hands and fret. Keep moving. Develop another game plan. God may even frustrate your next game plan—He may not want you to go into Bithynia. But don't get discouraged.

The hardest thing of all is when God seemingly puts you on the shelf and forbids you to preach the Word for a time. Can this possibly be God's will? It was for Paul.

So keep moving. Keep climbing those mountains through Mysia, and eventually you'll come to Troas.

Getting to Troas in those days was something like going today from Miami, Florida to Seattle, Washington. Tarsus, Paul's hometown, and Antioch of Syria, the location of Paul's home church, were in the far southeast. Troas was in the far northwest.

William Ramsey writes: "The natural development of Paul's work along the great central route of the Empire was forbidden, and the next alternative that rose in his mind was forbidden; he was led across Asia from the extreme southeast to the extreme northwest corner, and yet prevented from preaching in it; everything seemed dark and perplexing until at last a vision in Troas explained the purpose of this strange journey'' (*St. Paul the Traveller and Roman Citizen,* Baker, p. 190).

Alexander Maclaren writes, ''God sometimes tries patience and docility by making it abundantly clear what we are not to do, and leaving what we are to do absolutely dark. It takes much faith to acquiesce to such discipline'' (*The Acts of the Apostles,* Zondervan, p. 205).

Now Troas was a nice place to visit, but you wouldn't want to live there. It was a seaport town near the site of the legendary Troy, the scene of Homer's *Iliad*.

And when Paul and his companions got to Troas, they came to the Aegean Sea and could go no further without getting their feet wet. It looked as if the course they would have to take was backward—across the mountains of Mysia, back again to Galatia to drop off Timothy, and then back again to Antioch of Syria to report to the home church. But then what was God's purpose in all of this? Why did God lead them on this wild goose chase?

The Macedonian Vision

Then came what is referred to as the Macedonian Vision. Paul saw a vision of a man of Macedonia saying to him, ''Come over and help us.''

It was what the men had been waiting for. Immediately, they started to pack their bags. After wandering in confusion for several weeks, they now wasted no time in responding to this guidance.

It is interesting that although Paul had the vision, the decision to go was made by all of them: Paul, Silas, apparently Luke, and even Timothy (Acts 16:10). The weeks of uncertainty had molded Paul, Silas, and Timothy into a close-knit team. The word that is translated ''assuredly gathering'' in the King James Version really means "deducing by piecing things together." A.T. Robertson says it means "to make this and that agree and so to conclude." He calls it a "good illustration of the proper use of the reason in connection with revelation, to decide whether it is a revelation from God, to find out what it means for us, and to see that we obey the revelation when understood" (*Word Pictures in the New Testament,* Broadman). The same Greek word is also used to describe the way Paul put together Old Testament prophecies to prove that Jesus Christ was indeed God's promised Messiah.

You can almost picture the scene in Troas the morning after Paul had the vision. Perhaps it was at the breakfast table with Paul, Silas, Luke, and Timothy gathered around munching on bagels with cream cheese, or whatever first-century Jews ate at breakfast. Paul told of the strange vision that he'd had and asked for an evaluation from the others. Then gradually the men put two and two together. "Maybe this is why God didn't want us to go to Ephesus. . . . Maybe this is why we weren't allowed to go into Bithynia. . . . Maybe this is why we had to climb those Mysian mountains."

Now it all began to make sense. And it made such good sense that they may have skipped a second bagel that morning. They were too busy packing their bags.

And Timothy—he had to make a decision too. Was he willing to cross over the Aegean Sea and begin a new ministry? It would mean a longer separation from home and loved ones.

How about it, Timothy? Paul's vision had tied it all together. No one could doubt that it was the Lord's will.

Yes, it may have been more than Timothy had bargained for when he left home. But he was part of the team now and he couldn't turn back.

How to Conquer Macedonia

Macadam: a stone pavement.
Macadamia: a nut from Australia.
Macaque: a monkey from Asia.
Macaroni: a pasta from Italy.
Macassar: an oil from Indonesia.
Macaw: a parrot from Brazil.
Macédoine: a mixture of fruits.
Macedonia: an ancient country that nobody cares
about anymore.

Macedonia

Maybe the last definition is the one that comes to your mind, but you can be sure that young Timothy thought differently. Macedonia was the land from which Alexander the Great had come. Half Greek, Timothy must have heard the stories of Alexander's conquests from his father, just as he had heard the stories of Jewish heroes from his mother.

Going to Macedonia was like visiting Mount Vernon, Valley Forge, and Bunker Hill all at the same time. It brought to memory the noblest days of Greek conquest. So you can be sure that any young man with Greek blood in his veins would have looked forward to setting foot on Macedonian soil.

Of course, at this point Timothy would probably have been happy to go anywhere. The previous two months had been frustrating, to say the least. Everywhere Paul wanted to go, the Lord had said "No." Now it was different. God had said "Yes," and they were going.

The boat ride itself may have been a unique experience for Timothy. His hometown of Lystra was 100 miles from the Mediterranean Sea and 200 miles from the Aegean.

The Macedonian city to which they were headed was Philippi. Founded by Philip of Macedon (Alexander the Great's father), Philippi was the gold mining center that had supported Alexander's world conquest 400 years before Timothy was born. Less than 100 years before the Gospel arrived, Philippi was the site of an historic battle in which Octavian (later known as Augustus Caesar) and Antony defeated Brutus and Cassius. From that battle Augustus returned to Rome to take over the Empire; Brutus committed suicide.

Philippi was also a medical center in Macedonia, which may explain why Luke joined the missionary team at this point. At any rate, everyone seemed eager to get there. It seemed too that the Lord was eager to get them there. The boat ride, which sometimes took five days if the wind didn't cooperate, took only two days. After waiting for several weeks to get into action, the missionary troupe was now speeding into the fray.

Buoyed by the anticipation of finally getting into action, undergirded by the firm conviction that this was the place to which God had called them, and hyped by the romantic notions that must have permeated the land of Macedonia, the quartet—Paul, Silas, Timothy, and Luke—landed in the port of Neapolis and then began their 10-mile trek to the Roman colony of Philippi.

Arrival in Philippi

But what did they find when they got to Philippi? Nothing much. What a letdown!

When God leads you somewhere so clearly, shouldn't you expect a dramatic reception? Shouldn't the citizens be lined up on the beach waving palm branches? At least, couldn't you expect a huge synagogue in which to minister?

Well, that's not the way it worked, and halfway through the visit, Paul had good reason to wonder whether the Macedonian call had really come from the Lord after all.

Like Lystra, Philippi had no synagogue, indicating that there were only a few Jews in town. This meant that Paul was cut off from his most effective launching pad.

Once again, Paul had to search out the place where the worshipers of the true God met for prayer on the Sabbath. But it wasn't too hard to guess where that might be. Dispersed Jews often met along the banks of a river, in keeping with Psalm 137. A riverside was also a convenient location, in case any Gentiles wanted to be baptized.

Philippi's river, the Gangites, ran about a mile west of the city. This was where the four men found the worshipers of the true God. But as they surveyed the group, they noticed that there wasn't a man in the bunch. The worshipers were all women.

A Church of Women?

Could God establish a church here? Maybe the missionary troupe should go on to the next town. How could they establish a beachhead on the continent of Europe when all they had to work with was a handful of women?

It was a strange way to begin a European conquest. When Joshua crossed the Jordan and entered the Promised Land, he confronted the mighty walled city of Jericho. And when Jericho was taken, the rest of Canaan shook in its boots. But when Paul, Silas, Timothy, and Luke crossed the Aegean Sea and began their conquest of the Western world, they were confronted with a women's prayer meeting.

In our day when women are taking larger roles in society, we may miss a little of the humor of the situation. But for a rabbi who used to pray, "Lord, I thank Thee that Thou didst not make me a Gentile, a slave, or a woman," it was an ironic touch.

You can be sure that it also served as a reminder to Timothy. He had grown up under the tutelage of a concerned mother and grandmother. Philippi would always serve to remind him that a church—or a boy—nurtured by praying women will prosper.

Especially in Macedonia, Gentile women were attracted to Judaism. As in other cities, many of these women were appalled by the rampant immorality of society. Women were often the victims of crime and injustice. Besides that, it was easy for Gentile women to become proselytes to the Jewish faith. They merely had to be baptized, whereas men had to be circumcised. In addition, Macedonia afforded women more freedom and more civil rights than most cities. They exercised those rights by becoming active in business and in making their individual choices regarding religion. (Thus in both the Thessalonian and the Philippian churches, women were involved on the ground floor.)

After the riverside meeting ended, Paul had at least one convert—Lydia, who was a unique woman. A few years before, Jesus had sat down at a well in Samaria and a Samaritan woman had become a disciple. In Philippi, Paul sat down by a riverside and Lydia became a believer. But the comparison stops there. Lydia was a businesswoman from Thyatira in the province of Asia (where Paul, incidentally, had been forbidden by the Holy Spirit to preach). She sold expensive cloth of purple and prospered financially; in Philippi she had a dwelling large enough to provide hospitality for the four missionaries, as well as for her own household (which included servants as well as children).

At first the men seemed reluctant to take advantage of her hospitality. But as the Charles B. Williams translation of the New Testament puts it: "She begged us by continuing to say, 'If you have made up your mind that I am a real believer in the Lord, come and stay at my house.' And she continued to insist that we do so" (Acts 16:15).

So now they had a roof over their heads and they had made a convert, but thus far their "Macedonian campaign" was nothing to write home about. The prayer meetings became Scripture studies and instead of meeting every Sabbath, they began meeting every day. But they couldn't say that there was a revival going on. The congregation remained pretty much the same.

No great problems. No great results. Business as usual.

However, there was a minor irritation. A slave girl had made it a habit to follow the four men on their way down Philippi's Main Street, as they headed toward the morning Bible study. As she followed, she shrieked, "These men are slaves of God; they are telling us how to be saved."

It was a little like going down Main Street in your town with a PA system blaring out John 3:16.

It was more like the town drunk, lurching along with a

bottle of whiskey in his hand, inviting people to come to your church.

Every morning this slave girl called out the same words. At first, it may have seemed that the girl was only demented, but soon Paul sensed the girl was demon-possessed.

What were the missionaries to do? Before you answer, consider these two factors:

1. As the group went out to the riverside each day, they passed through a famous Philippian arch on which was an inscription forbidding foreign deities from entering the city. Normally, Philippi was a freedom-loving city that didn't pay much attention to the ban on foreign religions. But something had happened in Rome recently.

2. In the year A.D. 49, the Emperor Claudius had expelled all Jews from Rome because of a ruckus raised in the Jewish community. Certain Jews had been proclaiming that the Messiah had come. The turmoil over the issue had become so intense that the emperor kicked out all Jews. The Roman colony of Philippi was on the alert in case any members of the small Jewish community there got out of hand.

The next morning, the slave girl was following them again. Whatever her motivation, she needed help. She had called the missionaries slaves of God, but she herself was a slave of men who were profiting from her demonic gifts. She said that the missionaries were telling people how they could find a way of deliverance and liberation, and yet no one needed deliverance more than she did.

Liberation Action

Then Paul got involved. Angrily, he turned to rebuke the evil spirit: "I command you in the name of Jesus Christ to come out of her!" (Acts 16:18, NASB) It did and she was liberated from the oppressive spirit.

She was free, but soon Paul and Silas were not. They were cast into prison for interfering with business, for disturbing the peace, and for bringing religion into the streets of Philippi. (Timothy and Luke were not imprisoned, perhaps because they were not full-blooded Jews.)

Yet while Paul and Silas were placed in the inner prison and had their feet fastened into wooden stocks, they didn't let their spirits be chained. In prison, their singing provided entertainment for the other prisoners. In fact, they sang up an earthquake, and then the jailer asked how he could be liberated.

Funny thing, this matter of liberation. The man whose profession it was to keep people in chains found out that he was the one who needed deliverance. On the verge of committing suicide (that's what Brutus had done in Philippi), the jailer was stopped in the act by Paul and Silas. So he asked them—two prisoners—how he could be set free.

Strange things were going on in Philippi that night.

Philippi was a city proud of its Roman citizenship that guaranteed freedom to its people. But were the citizens of Philippi really free? Years later, Paul wrote the Philippians and told them about a heavenly citizenship, the only citizenship that could guarantee complete freedom (Phil. 3:20).

Was the jailer free? Obviously not. He bound others, but could not free himself.

What about Paul and Silas in the stocks? They were free. In fact, they were among the most liberated people in town. That's why they could sing!

About 100 years ago the Scottish preacher George Matheson wrote:

> Make me a captive, Lord
> And then I shall be free

Force me to render up my sword
And I shall conqueror be.
I sink in life's alarm
When in myself I stand;
Imprison with Thy mighty arm,
Then strong shall be my hand.

My heart is weak and poor,
Until it Master finds;
It has no spring of action sure,
It varies with the winds.
It cannot freely move
Till Thou hast wrought its chain.
Enslave it with Thy mighty love
Then deathless I shall reign.

Prison Break

Timothy must have been amazed how fast things were happening. For several weeks life had been rather humdrum in Philippi. Then within a 24-hour period, everything broke loose. He must have been reminded of a similar time in Lystra only a few years earlier.

Timothy was in Lydia's home with Dr. Luke, no doubt praying for the deliverance—there's that word again—of Paul and Silas. Probably, there were other believers also praying that night in Lydia's house. At least, they were there the next morning, when a knock came at the door. Paul and Silas entered the house and comforted and encouraged the brethren.

Well, it wouldn't have taken many words to comfort and encourage the brethren that morning. The word *comforted* is that delightful Greek word also used to refer to the Holy Spirit as the Comforter, the One "called alongside to help." Luke used the word another time in the

Book of Acts, when he spoke of Eutychus being restored to life in Troas, the brethren being "not a little comforted," a typical understatement of Dr. Luke. The Christians in Lydia's home were "not a little comforted" either as Paul and Silas were restored to them.

If the mere presence of Paul and Silas wasn't enough encouragement, the two men told the fantastic story of how they were singing in prison, with all the prisoners listening, when an earthquake loosened all of their chains. The jailer became so distraught that he was about to commit suicide. Paul and Silas calmed him and then told him about Jesus Christ. The jailer was saved and took the missionaries to his house, where his whole household believed. Within a few hours, when the town fathers learned that Paul and Silas were Roman citizens, they came in person to beg the two missionaries to leave the jail and get out of town. And that is when Paul and Silas stopped at Lydia's house.

Timothy's Training

For young Timothy, Philippi was a thrilling beginning of his ministry. Paul hadn't as yet written Romans 8:28, which speaks of how God works everything together for good to them that love Him, but already Timothy had experienced this truth.

How discouraged those young Philippian Christians must have been the night before when they first went down on their knees in prayer. But they had learned that God delights in serendipitous surprises. Philippi became a rejoicing church, and the letter that Paul later wrote to them is filled with joy.

One of the surprises in Philippi was the unlikely group that God brought together to form that infant church. John Drane describes it this way: "They came from all levels of society and included a prominent local trader, a soothsayer who looked for business in the main streets, and the town's jailer and his family. Small wonder that at one of the places they visited, Paul, Silas, and Timothy were described as men who turned the world upside down!'' (*Paul: An Illustrated Documentary,* Harper and Row, p. 61).

So often when we read Acts 16, we focus on the 31st verse, ''And they said, 'Believe in the Lord Jesus, and you shall be saved, you and your household''' (NASB). We look at Paul, Silas, and the jailer and tend to think that those three were the only ones affected.

But don't forget what a profound effect that experience must have had on the future life of young Timothy. This was the first body of believers he had helped to develop. While the faithful teaching of the Word day by day down by the riverside must have contributed greatly to the stability of the young church, the impetus for future growth came from those dramatic 24 hours which were planned and executed by Almighty God, not Paul. Man proposes, but God disposes. At Philippi, Timothy learned that the key to church growth is God Himself.

Persecution would come, as Paul had predicted when he visited Lystra years earlier. This time it had struck Paul and Silas; maybe next time Timothy would be in the middle of it. But the lesson that Timothy learned from watching Paul amid the persecution at Philippi was that Christians must learn not to be victimized by distress and tribulation. Instead they must transform those moments into opportunities.

Timothy must have wondered, as I would wonder, *If I were thrown into prison unjustly, would I be able to sing in the middle of the night? Or would I sulk and complain to God about why He had treated me so unjustly? Would I feel I was being punished for past mistakes? Would I focus on myself or would I look to God and say, ''Lord, I*

*don't know why You put me here, but I see some prison-
ers in the dim dankness around me and while I am waiting for Your next move, I might as well witness to them in
song''?*

God at Work

God is at work, Timothy; don't forget it. He's working
through you, even when you don't realize it. He is working during the early days at Philippi when things seem
humdrum and all you are doing is waking up early in the
morning, trudging outside the city walls to a riverside,
and telling a few ladies about Jesus Christ. He is working
even when the city's leaders take your two best
friends and cruelly beat them. He is working even when
you are praying in Lydia's house and an earthquake
frightens you out of your wits. (How are you supposed to
know what God has in mind to accomplish through His
earthquake down at the city jail?) But God is working;
don't forget it. And God is working when He draws together some of the most unlikely people in the world and
decides to make them into a model church. Yes, Timothy, God is working.

Do you remember that prayer that Paul and all the
rabbis prayed—''Lord, I thank Thee that Thou didst
not make me a Gentile, a slave, or a woman''?

Do you remember the first convert in Philippi—a
woman, and a liberated one, at that?

Do you remember the second convert—a slave, and
a demon-possessed girl, at that?

And do you remember the third convert—a Gentile, a
Roman jailer? That's the way God sometimes does
things, Timothy.

Conquest

I don't know what kind of Macedonian conquest Timothy had in mind when he set foot on the homeland of Alexander the Great. But by the time he left Philippi, he had learned some important lessons in discipleship:

> Make me a captive, Lord
> And then I shall be free.
> Force me to render up my sword
> And I shall conqueror be.

6

The Inventor of Shuttle Diplomacy

Do you think Henry Kissinger invented "shuttle diplomacy"? You're wrong. It was Timothy, back in A.D.50-51.

It all began in Thessalonica. The missionary quartet was now a trio, since Luke had stayed in Philippi to stabilize the church there. Evicted from Philippi, Paul, Silas, and Timothy hiked down the main highway about 100 miles to Thessalonica, a three-day walk. The main highway was Via Egnatia, the Route 66 of the Roman Empire; its connection in Italy was the Appian Way.

Since Thessalonica is quite important in Timothy's shuttle diplomacy, you'd better learn a little about it. Like Philippi, it was in the province of Macedonia, but it was bigger, brassier, and much more commercial. Paul's missionary game plan called for stops only in strategic cities—cities from which the Gospel would be spread to surrounding areas. He passed through two good-sized cities along the way from Philippi, but he stopped in Thessalonica because it was Macedonia's capital, because it had a Jewish synagogue, and because it was a hub from which to spread the Gospel.

Today a professional athlete may want to get traded to a team in New York City or Los Angeles, not necessarily to get on a pennant-winning team, but because of other advantages those cities provide for an athlete's career. Thessalonica was a city which provided "extra advantages."

Work in Philippi had been slow going. The missionaries had spent about three months there, and until the final days, progress had been slight. Three months may not seem very long to establish a church, but Paul was a man in a hurry. He was about 50 years old now, and the way things were going for him, he wasn't sure if he would reach 51, let alone 60.

In Philippi, Timothy had seen how a church could be planted in a city that didn't have a large Jewish population. But he could also see what an advantage it would have been for those new Christians if they had known the Old Testament promises of a Messiah.

Thessalonica, with a larger Jewish population, might be a different story. No doubt Paul was planning for a longer stay in the capital city of the province, hoping that it would be the hub for the evangelization of all Macedonia. With a population of 200,000, Thessalonica was the biggest city Paul had yet visited on his missionary journeys, and may have been the biggest city that Timothy had ever seen.

Thessalonica

"With overland caravans thronging its hostelries, with its harbor filled with ships' bottoms from overseas, with old salts, Roman officials, and thousands of Jewish merchants rubbing shoulders on its streets, Thessalonica presented a very cosmopolitan picture" (*Wycliffe Historical Geography of Bible Lands,* Moody, p. 457).

That's the kind of city Paul liked—a strategic city, a springboard city. The Gospel would easily spread from a city like that. Besides, Paul had received a special Macedonian call to evangelize the area, and Thessalonica was the logical place for his headquarters.

To get down to business, Paul did two things: He looked up a synagogue, and he set up shop as a tentmaker. If he was going to stay in Thessalonica for a while, he, Silas, and Timothy would have to have some bread on the table.

Paul's credentials as a rabbi were good, and so he was allowed to teach the Old Testament Scriptures on Sabbath morning in the synagogue. Paul probably began with Moses and the Prophets and explained how Jesus was the fulfillment of all the Old Testament Scriptures. As usual, the Resurrection was a key point in Paul's message. It was probably a standard message he used as he entered a synagogue in each new city he visited. If you want more details, look at his message in the synagogue of Antioch of Pisidia. (See Acts 13:14-41.)

Self-supporting Missionaries

During the week, the missionary trio apparently worked together as tentmakers, although it is possible that Silas and Timothy were trained in other crafts and found employment separately.

Paul told the Thessalonians, "Surely you remember, brothers, our toil and hardship; we worked night and day in order not to be a burden to anyone while we preached the Gospel of God to you" (1 Thes. 2:9, NIV). When Paul says, *we,* he is including Timothy. J.B. Phillips translates *toil and hardship* as *struggles and hard work.* Evidently, their lives were no picnic.

This was an aspect of discipleship that Timothy hadn't experienced before. Hadn't he been called of God to minister the Word of God with Paul? Why was he making tents instead? Was that in his job description? Isn't tentmaking a bit unspiritual?

Paul explained it to the Thessalonians as he must have explained it to young Timothy. For one thing, Paul had to make tents in order to eat. For another thing, the alternative was to ask the young Thessalonian church to support the trio. While there would be nothing wrong with that, at this stage of the game Paul felt it would be unwise.

But there was a third reason. Paul said, "We loved you so much that we were delighted to share with you not only the Gospel of God, but our lives as well" (1 Thes. 2:8, NIV). They shared by living and working with the people, and by serving the people in menial work.

Wouldn't it have been better if they could have preached full time? Maybe. But maybe not. A disciple needs to learn that the Gospel is presented in more ways than in direct proclamation.

Rabbi Jehuida said, "He who does not teach his son a trade is much the same as if he taught him to be a thief." Paul's own mentor Gamaliel once said, "He that has a craft in his hands, unto what is he like? He is like a vineyard that is fenced." In other words, it is good insurance for a rabbi to know how to do something besides teach.

What we call *secular work* is good not only as a means to an end, but it is also good in itself. Making tents was a way that Paul and the other missionaries could serve the Thessalonians; it was similar to what Jesus had in mind when He washed the disciples' feet. And work was a way the men could share in the sweat and everydayness of the lives of the people to whom they were ministering spiritually.

As hard as it was, tentmaking and synagogue teaching combined to make a winning combination. Timothy must have been excited to see the variety of new converts. They included "some of the Jews . . . a large number of God-fearing Greeks," and "not a few prominent women" (Acts 17:4, NIV).

Trouble Brewing

But Timothy's excitement was short-lived. Trouble was brewing and he could smell it. The first clue was that they were no longer welcome to teach in the synagogue. Apparently, the three men continued their ministry in the streets and in the homes, primarily in the home of their host, Jason. When some of the Gentile converts stopped going to the synagogues in favor of the Christian meetings, that stirred up more trouble.

Tension was mounting. Timothy must have had that "here we go again" feeling. In Lystra, Timothy had seen Paul stoned. In Philippi, the first real stop of this missionary trip, Timothy had seen Paul and Silas beaten and hauled off to prison. And now in Thessalonica the atmosphere was charged. What was going to happen this time?

The leaders of the synagogue felt that Paul and Company were not only stealing their sheep, but depriving them of some offerings. When some of the well-to-do Gentile women began going to Christian worship instead of to the Jewish synagogue, it hit the synagogue leaders in the pocketbook. And that hurt.

So, aided by a gang of rowdies who hung around the city market, they fomented a riot and descended on the home of Jason where Paul, Silas, and Timothy were staying. Unfortunately for the gang, the missionaries weren't home. So poor Jason was dragged to court and charged—along with the absent missionaries—with subversion, sedition, and disorderly conduct.

It seems too bad that Paul never added a lawyer to his missionary team. In almost every chapter in the latter half of the Book of Acts, he could have used one. In this case, Jason needed one too.

The charges brought against Paul, Silas, Timothy, and Jason were serious indeed. As F.F. Bruce stated, "It could not be denied that, more often than not, his (Paul's) coming to any city was a prelude to rioting and, in particular, that the Jesus whom he proclaimed as sovereign Lord had been executed by sentence of a Roman court on a charge of claiming to be King of the Jews" (*Apostle of the Heart Set Free,* Eerdmans, p. 226).

No one could deny the charge that Christianity was turning the world upside down.

However, Timothy was hardly the kind of fellow that you would seriously charge with such a major offense. "Cause a riot?" he might have asked. "My stomach does flip-flops when I have to talk to more than 10 people at once."

But when God is at work, He can use even a Timothy to overturn the world.

Well, the town fathers demanded Jason's guarantee that the missionaries would get out of town and cause no more trouble. Once again, the news of what had happened in Rome under Emperor Claudius must have caused the Thessalonian officials to run scared. Rather than investigate the trumped-up charges more carefully, they decided not to take any chances.

Escape to Berea

So that night, Paul, Silas, and Timothy left for Berea, 50 miles away. Their total stay in Thessalonica, including three weeks in the synagogue, was probably two or three months, though some Bible scholars stretch it to five. But for Paul it wasn't long enough.

You see, God had given him clear instructions to go to Macedonia, and Thessalonica was its capital city. He had received moving orders from the town officials, but he hadn't received them from God.

Besides that, the congregation they left behind was largely Gentile, many of whom had been worshiping idols not long before (see 1 Thes. 1:9). In other words, if you're having a revival in the capital city, you hate to be transferred to the boondocks. Souls in both places are precious, but the big city is much more strategic.

Berea was in the boondocks. No doubt, Paul was hoping that things would quiet down in Thessalonica in a few weeks and then the three men could return there and continue their ministry.

But things didn't quiet down in Thessalonica. So instead, a virile and Bible-loving church was founded in Berea. The trouble was that the news of what was going on in Berea got back to Thessalonica, and then the Thessalonian troublemakers went to Berea and brought some trouble with them.

Paul wasn't the type to run every time he came face to face with difficulty, and yet he recognized that sometimes it was in the best interests of the local church for him to get out of the way as quickly as possible.

Escape to Athens

Paul was the irritant, the pesky fly that Thessalonian agitators were determined to swat. So the best thing for him to do was head south.

It's doubtful whether he told anyone where he was going. In fact, maybe Paul wasn't sure himself when he left Berea. His first thought was probably to go to Thessaly, only about 100 miles south. But his Berean escorts convinced him to go farther, so he traveled about 200 miles south to Greece's intellectual and cultural capital, Athens. Timothy and Silas, however, stayed in Berea, ministering to the church there, watching the situation in Thessalonica to see if the political and emotional climate would change, and awaiting new instructions from Paul.

If Timothy had the notion that he was simply going to be a management trainee under the watchful eye of his boss Paul throughout the missionary journey, that notion was being rapidly dispelled. More and more Timothy had to operate on his own. Close to a year had now passed since he had joined Paul's team. That would put his age at 20 or 21. But he was being thrust into significant responsibility already.

Probably, it took about two weeks for Timothy and Silas to get word from Paul that he wanted the two of them to join him in Athens as soon as they could. No doubt he also asked them to bring word on the Thessalonian situation. Was it safe to return yet? Had the situation cooled down?

The word that Timothy and Silas took to Paul was that things were getting worse, not better in Thessalonica. If Paul went back, it would only aggravate the situation.

It may have been that there was some thought of terminating the second missionary journey at this point, with Timothy perhaps returning to Lystra and Paul and Silas returning to Antioch of Syria. But there was too much unfinished business. The three of them had spent a year traveling and had started three churches, but each of these churches had been left in haste. How could Paul report back to the church of Antioch with any accuracy? After his first journey, he had doubled back and revisited each church, and he had been encouraged with progress in Lystra, Iconium, and Antioch. But on this second journey, Thessalonica had been his key stop, and he couldn't revisit it.

Paul had sung songs in a Philippian prison, but in the Athenian sunshine he seemed discouraged. How much had really been accomplished in the past year? They had heeded the Macedonian call, but all they had gotten for their efforts was trouble.

There was only one thing that could be done. Since Paul couldn't retrace his steps this time (some say it may have been because of a recurring illness, but more probably it was because of the political situation), he would have to send Timothy and Silas back to get a firsthand assessment of the situation.

Timothy to Thessalonica

So Timothy was sent back to turbulent Thessolonica, while Silas was dispatched to Philippi or possibly to Berea. Why was Timothy sent to the more troublesome spot?

Perhaps Timothy would not have been considered the threat to the agitators that Silas as prophet and teacher would have been. Perhaps Silas had been more visible in synagogue preaching than Timothy, who was only half Jewish. At any rate, Timothy got the job.

It's obvious that it was only Paul's great concern for the Thessalonians that caused him to dispatch his "son in the faith" to the hot spot of Thessalonica. He wrote to them: "We wanted to come to you—I, Paul, more than once—and yet Satan thwarted us. . . . Therefore when we could endure it no longer, we thought it best to be left behind at Athens alone; and we sent Timothy, our brother and God's fellow-worker in the Gospel of Christ, to strengthen and encourage you as to your faith" (1 Thes. 2:18; 3:1-2, NASB).

Timothy's 200-mile trek back to Thessalonica would have taken seven days of walking and thinking and praying. Timothy must have wondered if he would be walking into a den of lions, as Daniel did. But Timothy was no Daniel by temperament. Nor had he the boldness of

Peter, nor the bravery of David.

He may have been shaking in his boots for the entire 200 miles, but he kept on walking—and thinking—but probably mostly praying.

His job in Thessalonica was not simply to be a reporter, picking up tidbits of news, sneaking furtively through the city without anyone seeing him. His job was to strengthen the church there. It was as if a tree had been transplanted and now Timothy needed to attach some cords and stake it down so it wouldn't be blown over by the violent winds. The work needed to be buttressed.

Now you may think that Timothy himself needed to be buttressed, that perhaps he needed some guy wires so he wouldn't be blown over. But God doesn't always call on the strong to support the weak; sometimes He calls on you and in the process you become stronger yourself.

What would Timothy say to the people? Only a few years before, his home church in Lystra had been in a similar situation. The townspeople had stoned Paul and run him out of town, but a few weeks later he had returned, "confirming the souls of the disciples, and exhorting them to continue in the faith," for they would "through much tribulation enter into the kingdom of God" (Acts 14:22). That was a message that Timothy would never forget. And it would be a message especially appropriate for Thessalonica.

Barclay likens Timothy to a postage stamp. He says, "One of the special things about Timothy is that time and time again we read about Paul sending him somewhere. In fact, Timothy must have spent most of his life going on expeditions on which Paul sent him." And then Barclay points out why Timothy was such a good messenger. It was because he was like a postage stamp. "The postage stamp sticks to its job. It is stuck on the envelope and there it stays until it has reached its destination. The person who lets the difficulties beat him never arrives anywhere. A good messenger never gives up until he has delivered his message.

"Second, the postage stamp goes where it is sent. Stick it on the envelope and it will go to Edinburgh, or London, to Paris, or Berlin, to Peking, or Timbuctoo. . . . The trouble with most people is that they will work their hardest and their best at the things they like doing, and will do practically nothing to the things they do not like doing. . . . It did not matter to Timothy where he was sent. He went. It was enough for him that Paul wanted him to go. . . . One of the great tests of any person is if he can really put his back into things that he does not want to do" (*God's Young Church,* Westminster, p. 105).

How long Timothy stayed in Thessalonica on his fact-finding mission is unknown. Most scholars think it was probably several weeks. During that time, besides teaching, he was assessing the situation for Paul.

What he found was mostly on the positive side. However, there were problems, persecutions, and pressures. The young Christian church was persecuted by both Jews and Gentiles. To complicate matters, the Jewish leaders exercised more subtle pressure: "If you come back and join us, you will avoid all the persecution you're now getting." But despite the problems, the Christians in the young church weren't letting the situation get them down. Their Christian example was known from Philippi to Athens. Their lives were a vivid contrast to their contemporaries—it wasn't easy to live a moral life in Thessalonica.

In his commentary, William Neil states, "The fact is that one of the most difficult hurdles that any pagan convert had to clear was the Christian attitude toward sex. He had been brought up in a world where polygamy, concubinage, homosexuality, and promiscuity were accepted as a matter of course. . . . Many of the religious cults were frankly sexual in character, with phallic rites and sacramental fornication as part of their worship" (*Acts*, Attic Press).

That the converts in Thessalonica were able to live upright lives in such an immoral world was proof that the Holy Spirit could keep new converts on the straight and narrow, without the crutch of legalism. If Timothy had any second thoughts about the rightness of Paul's argument in the Letter to the Galatians, they would have been dispelled by what he witnessed on this fact-finding trip to Thessalonica.

Now I don't mean to say that the newborn Christians were vaccinated against falling into sin. Nor do I mean to imply that they didn't have any problems. But their basic problem was that they were babes in Christ.

As the old Gospel chorus goes, "They had the joy, joy, joy, joy, down in their hearts." They even had the "love of Jesus, love of Jesus, down in their hearts." But they didn't have the Word of God down in their hearts, yet.

To Timothy, their faith probably seemed shallow. The Thessalonian Christians were living on an emotional level. They hadn't had time for their faith to put down deep roots. They had had no teachers to instruct them.

Their leaders hadn't earned their confidence yet. The people had questions that their leaders couldn't answer. And apparently they didn't trust the answers of 20-year-old Timothy, either. Most of their unanswered questions had to do with the second coming of Christ. Apparently, they had learned just enough to know that Jesus Christ would come back, but not enough to know how that truth applied to daily living in the here and now. (And that's not a problem restricted to churches in the first century.)

They also didn't understand what happens to those who die before Christ returns. *Would the dead miss out on the blessings of the Second Coming?* they wondered.

Back to Athens

So when Timothy headed down south again to report to Paul, he had a lot to tell him. Apparently, Timothy went to Paul's last known address in Athens, and discovered that he had moved. Timothy was pointed in the direction of Corinth.

Today when we think of Greece, Athens is the first city that comes to mind. But in Paul's day, Athens was number two and on its way down. Its golden years of glory were 300 years in the past. Athens was still known for education, philosophy, and culture, but Corinth had long ago surpassed it in every other way. The Athenians were better at thinking and talking than they were at doing. The Corinthians were good at talking and doing, but often not good at thinking.

What Thessalonica was to the province of Macedonia, and what Ephesus was to the province of Asia, Corinth was to Achaia, the province that comprised southern Greece. So, if Timothy thought much about it, he would not have been too surprised that Paul's new address was another strategic city, the capital of Achaia.

When Timothy found Paul in the tentmaker's section of the Corinthian market, he may have been surprised at Paul's mental state. In his biography of Paul, F.F. Bruce says, "Paul traveled from Athens to Corinth in a mood of dejection. It had probably been no part of his program when he crossed the sea to Macedonia to turn south into the province of Achaia. But he had been driven from one Macedonian city after another, and it seemed that, for the time being, there was no place for him in that province, despite his previous assurance that God had called him to evangelize it. True, his preaching in Macedonia had not been fruitless; he had left small groups of converts behind him in Philippi, Thessalonica, and Berea. But his mind was full of misgivings about their well-being. . . . Athens had been much less encouraging than the cities of Macedonia. So he arrived in Corinth, as he says, 'in weakness and in fear and in much trembling' '' (1 Cor. 2:3, NASB, in *Apostle of the Heart,* p. 248).

Granted, by this time Paul had found Priscilla and Aquila, two Christian immigrants from Rome, who must have done his spirits a world of good. But the big burden on Paul's heart was still the state of the Christians up north.

What an encouragement it must have been when both Timothy and Silas returned from Thessalonica and Philippi with good news! Silas also brought a gift from the Philippian church (2 Cor. 11:9), which enabled Paul to devote full time to preaching and teaching.

The First Thessalonian Letter
But first, he had to write a letter to the Thessalonians. Apparently, Silas' report from Philippi did not indicate that the Philippian Christians needed a letter at this time. (Perhaps Luke was still there helping the young congregation.) But the Thessalonian Christians, going through persecution and puzzled by several knotty questions, needed a letter post haste.

So Paul began writing his first letter to the Thessalonian church. Because both Silas and Timothy had been his co-laborers in Thessalonica and because they were now at his side in Corinth as he penned the letter, he included their names in the salutation. It does not mean that Timothy wrote one third of the letter, but it does indicate the high regard Paul had for this 20-year-old son in the faith.

Later in the epistle (1 Thes. 3:2), Paul referred to this young man as "our brother, and minister of God, and our fellow-laborer in the Gospel of Christ."

Remember that Timothy had been an intern on Paul's missionary team for slightly more than a year; remember too that Timothy was not a dominant youth. He wouldn't have won letters in all sports at the Lystra high school, or earned high honors at a university. Yet Paul regarded him as an equal.

It is difficult to make the transition from son to brother. In some churches youth seldom have a chance to make meaningful contributions. But Paul did not jealously guard his position. If he could spread the responsibility to a younger generation, so much the better.

In the first part of his Thessalonian letter (chapters 1—3), he reminded the Thessalonians of what had gone on in the previous six months. It was an emotional letter, written from the heart of a man whose depression had just been transformed into deep satisfaction. He told them how Timothy, his co-worker (some versions use the phrase "co-worker with God"), had brought back a glowing commendation of their spiritual progress. He referred to it as *good news,* the only time in the New Testament where *good news* does not refer specifically to the Gospel of salvation. Paul told them how Timothy's report had cheered him up. "Now I'm living," Paul said. "Thanks for the joy you have given me." (See 1 Thes. 3:8-9.) Paul was emotionally involved in the welfare of his spiritual children.

I wonder if someone looked at the spiritual progress you and I have made in the past six months, if he would feel very much joy.

The Second Coming
In the last section of the short epistle, Paul reminded the

church of the necessity of sexual purity, the importance of church leaders, and the implications of the Second Coming.

The Second Coming doesn't mean that we should quit our jobs, climb to the top of Mount Olympus, and wait for Christ to come again. It doesn't mean that we should get out our prophecy charts and do nothing while the poor are starving in Bangladesh and the Western world is threatening to blow itself to smithereens with atom bombs. Nor does it mean that those who have died are going to miss out on blessings. They are going to be resurrected first, and we will be meeting them in the clouds when the Lord comes back.

So, Paul said, "Of course, you will grieve when a loved one dies, but you don't have to grieve as those who don't have any hope. Cheer up one another with these words." (See 1 Thes. 4:13-18.)

And the Second Coming also means that we should always be ready and not be taken by surprise, because when Jesus comes, He will come suddenly.

Paul knew he hadn't said all there was to say about the Second Coming, but he hoped it would be enough to answer the questions of the young Thessalonian Christians.

Did Timothy deliver this letter to the Thessalonians? We don't know. It would seem, however, that if Timothy were to engage in more shuttle diplomacy, Paul would have referred to it in either 1 or 2 Thessalonians. Probably, Paul used a courier this time and kept both Timothy and Silas with him at Corinth.

Encouraging Friends

One might think that Paul was a man who didn't need friends, but it's obvious from his epistles that his ministry was more effective when he had co-workers around him. When Paul was alone, he sometimes became depressed. There was something encouraging about Timothy; when he was around, Paul became a better missionary.

In Exodus 17 is the story of a battle between the Children of Israel and the Amalekites. It was a strange battle. Joshua was the general, fighting at the battlefront. Moses was on a hilltop with the rod of God in his hand. But two other men were also involved: Aaron and Hur. When Moses lifted up his hands, Joshua went forward; when Moses tired and dropped his hands, Joshua retreated. That's when Aaron and Hur got into the act. They raised Moses' hands for him and the battle was won.

Timothy and Silas were like Aaron and Hur. They kept Paul's arms uplifted. Everyone knows about the Apostle Paul, just as everyone knows about Moses. But behind the scenes were Timothy and Silas, and Aaron and Hur, encouraging, supporting, facilitating, troubleshooting, and engaging in shuttle diplomacy. As a result, spiritual battles were won.

Timothy would return to Thessalonica later, the next time as an advance man for Paul. But for now he stayed with Paul.

At the age of 20, Timothy had proven to be faithful and successful in shuttle diplomacy. Certainly, this must have given him great encouragement.

Frankly, he would need it, for the most difficult test of his Christian life was coming up soon.

How to Triumph While Flunking

You can give Timothy an *E* for effort, if you please. But to be honest, you'll have to give him an *F* for failure.

You know the feeling. You may remember slouching through the front door with an F on your report card, laying the card on the table underneath the newspaper, and then hoping that no one would pay any attention to it. You may remember typing the important letter for the boss, proofreading it carefully, and then proudly presenting it to him for his signature, only to have him find four misspellings. That's the feeling.

Of course, there are extenuating circumstances. In any failure, there *always* seems to be a string of extenuating circumstances.

Corinth

For one thing, you've got to understand Corinth. Corinth was an extenuating circumstance if you ever saw one. If Athens resembled Boston with its history, culture, and education, then Corinth resembled San Francisco, Los Angeles, San Diego, and Las Vegas all rolled into one.

95

(You can add a little dash of Chicago to round it out.)

Its population was probably close to a half million, but Corinthians seldom stayed in one place long enough to be counted. For all practical purposes, Corinth was less than 100 years old and growing like an adolescent. In some ways, it was more Roman than Greek; but to be more proper, it was more *everything* than *anything*.

Corinth was a sailor town, a wide open town, a transient and commercial seaport, a crossroads between East and West, a cosmopolitan and a sports-loving town. It was known around the world for its immorality and for its Isthmian Games (a rival of the Olympics). Anyone staying in its streets long enough would hear the jabbering of a dozen different languages.

Located 50 miles west of Athens and 50 miles east of Delphi, Corinth was jealous of both, like a middle sibling. It pretended to have Athens' wisdom and Delphi's religious clout, but it had neither.

As E.M. Blaiklock says, "Vicious, prosperous, without deep roots in tradition, the people of Corinth were too ready, with the facility of immigrant communities, to adopt the vices rather than the virtues of the land of their adoption" (*Bible Characters and Doctrines,* Col. XIV, Eerdmans, p. 12).

The Isthmian Games, of which the Corinthians were so proud, did not offer laurel wreaths to its winners, but wreaths made out of wild celery stalks. No wonder Paul told the Corinthians to be wary of seeking a "corruptible crown" (1 Cor. 9:25).

When Timothy, the small-town youth from Lystra, arrived in Corinth, Paul had already been preaching there for several weeks. As usual, Paul had begun in the local synagogue. But shortly after Timothy arrived, Paul was kicked out. So he moved next door to the house of one of his new converts and continued preaching.

Well, you can imagine how the synagogue leaders liked that. Another riot. As usual.

This time, however, the provincial governor Gallio, brother of the famed Roman philosopher Seneca, saw through the trumped-up charges of the synagogue leaders. As a result Paul, Silas, and Timothy were able to continue their evangelistic work in Corinth.

Three Encouragements

But it wasn't easy. At times, it seemed as if the whole work would go down the drain. Once, shortly after they had been evicted from the synagogue, God gave Paul a special vision and told him not to be afraid "for I have much people in this city" (Acts 18:10). Timothy probably needed that encouragement too.

Sometimes discouragement comes because we cannot see as far ahead as God can. It's like driving on a foggy night; we're afraid to move ahead and afraid to stand still. We pray and we see nothing happening. We work and things keep getting worse. At such times we wish that God would give us a vision as he gave Paul.

Earlier, of course, Paul had been told by God to go to Macedonia where the cities of Philippi and Thessalonica were, but he had never been given orders to go to Achaia where the cities of Athens and Corinth were located. He felt he had been forced there by satanic obstacles that kept him from returning to Macedonia. So even as Paul preached and made tents in Corinth, his heart was still in Thessalonica.

The vision wasn't simply to encourage Paul, but also to assure him that he was in the right place. Paul needed to be reassured that he was in the center of God's will.

A second source of encouragement for Paul was the return of Timothy and Silas from their errands up north. They not only encouraged him with good news on how the churches were faring, but also took over some duties, enabling him to devote his time to preaching and teaching, instead of tentmaking.

Speaking about tentmaking leads us to Paul's third source of encouragement: Priscilla and Aquila, a unique husband and wife team who kept popping up in strategic places throughout Paul's missionary journeys. Some New Testament scholars suggest that they may have owned a chain of tentmaking shops in Rome, Corinth, and Ephesus (the McDonalds of the tentmaking world). Ejected from Rome by Emperor Claudius, Priscilla and Aquila moved to their Corinthian franchise, arriving there just before Paul hiked into the city. They no doubt filled Paul in on the status of the Christian church in Rome. But besides that, they gave him a job and Christian companionship when he desperately needed both.

Usually God doesn't give visions to encourage us; more often He sends people—people like Timothy and Silas, Priscilla and Aquila—to give the encouragement needed in our times of discouragement.

Timothy had been living out of a suitcase for the past year and a half, and his toga probably needed a thorough dry cleaning. But from the looks of the situation around Corinth, he probably didn't feel that he would be able to unpack there either. Despite problems and discouragements, however, the Corinthian stop proved to be one of the longest that Paul ever made, a total of 18 months. During that time, Timothy watched the church grow rapidly. Although Corinth was the moral cesspool of the ancient world, the church there became one of the largest in the early church period. So there was much for Timothy to do. For instance, Paul mentioned that he personally baptized only a very few of the Corinthian converts (1 Cor. 1:14). That means that most of the baptisms were performed by Silas and Timothy.

Missionary Travels

It was probably in the spring of A.D. 52 that Paul, Timothy, and Silas concluded their missionary journey. Nearly three years had passed since Timothy had joined Paul and Silas in Lystra. If he was 19 when they had started, he was 22 now. During those three years he had done a lot of growing up.

On the way back home, the team stopped at Ephesus. It was the one remaining major city on the Aegean Gulf in which they had not as yet planted a church. Already Paul must have had in mind a third journey that would focus on Ephesus. To do some groundwork for his next missionary foray, he left Priscilla and Aquila in Ephesus. Then he and Silas boarded a ship and headed for Palestine.

Whether Timothy accompanied them is not known. My guess is that he used the time as a missionary furlough to return home to Lystra, to spend some time with his mother and grandmother.

That fall, the Apostle Paul traveled back through the Galatian cities on his way to Ephesus and probably picked up Timothy at Lystra. Silas wasn't with Paul this time, so Timothy, at the age of 22, became Paul's senior associate. When they got to Ephesus, Priscilla and Aquila were waiting for them.

For nearly three years, Paul ministered in Ephesus, getting in and out of trouble, which seemed to be par for the course whenever he evangelized a city. Some of the trouble is spelled out in Acts 19, but Luke didn't have room to include some of the "less significant" matters at Ephesus—things like fighting the wild beasts (1 Cor. 15:32); an imprisonment or two (Rom. 16:7; 2 Cor. 11:23-27); Priscilla and Aquila "risking their necks for him" (Rom. 16:4); and his escape from peril of death (2 Cor. 1:10).

How many of these problems involved Timothy is not known, but as number-two man in the organization you can be sure that he could say with Paul, "We were under great pressure, far beyond our ability to endure, so that we despaired even of life" (2 Cor. 1:8, NIV).

What was there in Timothy that made him come back for more? He had gone through one missionary journey with Paul; and after three or four months at home, he reenlisted for another term. If he had shared all his experiences with friends in Lystra and then told them he was volunteering for more, they would probably have said, "Timothy, you're crazy." And you can imagine the feelings of his mother Eunice.

Barnabas had gone with Paul on only one journey; Silas had gone with Paul on only one journey. But here was Timothy, the kid with the weak stomach, going for a second.

Of course, he could have changed his mind in Ephesus. After all, that's what John Mark had done, and Mark hadn't experienced a tenth of what Timothy had faced. Besides, Ephesus wasn't that far from home. He could easily have jumped aboard a camel train and gotten home in a few days. But he didn't, even though many times he must have felt "crushed and overwhelmed," as the *Living Bible* puts it, or "exceedingly depressed quite beyond endurance," as Weymouth expresses it (2 Cor. 1:8).

As usual, Timothy's role on Paul's team involved a lot of traveling. In baseball terminology, Timothy was Paul's designated hitter. It wasn't because Timothy could hit home runs, but rather that he would always make contact.

As I read the epistles, it seems to me that Timothy might have made two or three long trips during the time Paul had his headquarters in Ephesus. But the most significant one was the one that ended in failure, involving that troublesome city of Corinth. To understand what Timothy was up against, it's necessary to piece together all of Paul's correspondence to the Corinthian church. And "piece together" is the right phrase, for it is somewhat of a puzzle.

Corinthian Letters

Over a three-year period, Paul probably wrote four letters to the Corinthian church (it could be five). Scholars label these letters A, B, C, and D (and possibly E). We have two of them, letters B and D, which we call 1 and 2 Corinthians, and it's possible, as some scholars think, that 2 Corinthians is really C and D combined. In that case we have three of the four or five possible letters.

If the scholars are confused about it, don't feel embarrassed if all the pieces don't fit together perfectly for you either. Probably, it was a bit of a jigsaw puzzle for Timothy too.

We don't know how Paul first heard that there was trouble in Corinth, but the city was directly across the Aegean Sea from Ephesus and so news traveled normally between the two cities. Sailing time in good weather was only two to three days.

In his first letter (referred to in 1 Cor. 5:9), Paul warned against immorality. But Paul must have felt that the Corinthians needed more than a letter. And so to follow up letter A, he dispatched Timothy to Corinth. Timothy probably traveled the semicircle that would bring him in contact with Philippi and Thessalonica on his way to Corinth. (See 1 Cor. 4:17 and 16:10.) This would be a land trip of several hundred miles and probably would last two to three months.

Apparently, Paul's letter A was not too effective. At least, that's what "Chloe's people" (1 Cor. 1:11, NASB) told Paul when they appeared on his doorstep in Ephesus. They told him not only of immorality, but also that the church was breaking up into different parties (*minidenominations,* you might call them) and that Paul's authority was being questioned.

Before long, three other Corinthian members arrived, adding to the tale of woe that Chloe's people had brought. These three probably brought with them a letter asking a number of questions about matters that were disturbing the Corinthians.

Responding to all of this, Paul proceeded to write letter B, the letter we know as 1 Corinthians. We know that Timothy had already left town, because Paul did not include him in the salutation (1 Cor. 1:1).

In writing to the Corinthians, Paul tried to pave the way for Timothy's visit. He reminded the Corinthians (1 Cor. 4:14-17) that they were his children in the faith, and therefore should pay attention to their "spiritual father." Timothy was also a son in the faith and was faithful in the Lord, an example that Paul hoped his sons in Corinth would imitate. Timothy was sent by Paul to coach them especially in moral behavior, a lifestyle which Paul had been presenting in all the churches he had launched.

Near the end of the epistle, Paul told the Corinthians that he would be coming to visit them shortly, and was sending Timothy ahead of him. "See to it that he has nothing to fear," Paul wrote (1 Cor. 16:10, NIV). Paul did not fear for Timothy's physical safety as much as for his psychological safety. "Accept him," Paul said, "for he is doing the Lord's work as I am."

The problems in the Corinthian church would scare anyone, and probably Timothy didn't know what a hornet's nest he was confronting. He'd had no trouble in his previous troubleshooting mission with the Thessalonian church because they had accepted Paul's authority and had known that Timothy was Paul's faithful sidekick.

But the Corinthian situation was different. Many of the church members questioned Paul's right to give them orders; why should they listen to young Timothy?

Timothy, says William LaSor in *Great Personalities of the New Testament,* "had been sent to Corinth by Paul to take care of grave difficulties in that church, difficulties of a moral, doctrinal, and administrative nature. To read the letters to the Corinthians is to discover how complex the problems were" (Revell, p. 152).

Not only was the church divided into four minidenominations; it was also influenced by libertines, by legalists, by philosophers, and by mystics, all of whom interpreted the Christian message differently. And all of them seemed intensely proud (Paul uses the term *puffed up*) about their unique interpretations.

Whether the people even listened to Timothy is not known. But the fact is that he failed.

LaSor says, "He failed not because of any lack of ability, but because of lack of experience; he was just too young. The church in Corinth despised his youth and were hostile because Paul himself had not visited them" (*Great Personalities,* p. 152). It would seem that Timothy had made the situation worse and not better. Timothy then reported back to Paul the sad and sorry news.

Ever since meeting Paul, Timothy had gotten involved in things bigger than he was. He was always wading in water beyond his depth.

It could be that Paul dispatched Timothy to the Macedonian and Corinthian churches before he realized the enormity of the problems in Corinth. He may not have known that he was sending Timothy into a buzz saw. Timothy had performed well in his shuttle diplomacy with the church in Thessalonica. Why should he not do well in Corinth where Paul had spent 18 months preaching and teaching the Word of God?

When Timothy came back with the word that he had failed, Paul was quite incensed—not at Timothy, but at the Corinthians.

Many scholars feel that Paul himself took a quick trip, the "painful visit," to Corinth to see if he could settle the problems (2 Cor. 2:1, NIV). Evidently, even this was unsatisfactory, so he wrote a strong letter (letter C in the string of correspondence), and sent it with Titus. Afterward, he had second thoughts about it: *Maybe I was too harsh. Did I react emotionally to their shabby treatment of Timothy? Instead of settling anything, this letter may ruin everything. It may sever completely my relationship with the Corinthian church.*

Evidently, Paul had told Titus to report back to him in Troas (Troy), about 100 miles north of Ephesus. But when Paul and Timothy arrived in Troas, Titus wasn't there. At this point, both Paul and Timothy must have felt like failures. The fact that Titus hadn't returned when he was expected must have meant that letter C had not helped to untangle the situation in Corinth.

There were opportunities for evangelism in Troas, but Paul could not take advantage of them. He had no peace of mind (2 Cor. 2:13). So Paul and Timothy continued on to Philippi in Macedonia, still concerned over the fact that they had heard nothing from Titus. Paul's account tells it best: "Even after I had gotten to Macedonia, my frail, human nature could find no relief; I was crushed with sorrow at every turn—fightings without and fears within" (2 Cor. 7:5, WMS).

If that was the reaction of Paul—who later wrote to the Philippian church, "Don't worry about anything" (see Phil. 4:7)—think how Timothy must have been affected.

R.V.G. Tasker in his commentary on 2 Corinthians

states: "It is part of the frailty of human nature that it is subject to tensions and strains which have both mental and physical repercussions; and such strains are most acutely felt by hypersensitive souls such as Paul" (*II Corinthians,* Eerdmans, p. 103).

Success with Letters

Then Titus walked in the front door. Of this happy arrival, Paul later wrote: "But God, who comforts the downcast, comforted us by the coming of Titus, and not only by his coming but also by the comfort you had given him. He told us about your longing for me, your deep sorrow, your ardent concern for me, so that my joy was greater than ever" (2 Cor. 7:6-7, NIV).

Letter C had succeeded. Titus had succeeded. Paul and the Corinthians were reconciled. And now Paul was glad that he had sent letter C: "I caused you sorrow by my letter, I do not regret it; though I did regret it—for I see that that letter caused you sorrow, though only for a while—I now rejoice, not that you were made sorrowful, but that you were made sorrowful to the point of repentance" (2 Cor. 7:8-9, NASB).

Out of his great joy Paul then wrote letter D, which we call 2 Corinthians.

As Paul began this letter he wrote, "Paul, an apostle of Christ Jesus by the will of God, and Timothy our brother."

Surprising, isn't it?

Why not Paul and Titus? Titus had just come back with the good news; Titus was the one who had reestablished the relationship with the Corinthians; Titus was the one who had been successful.

Paul certainly appreciated what Titus had done. From this time on, Titus came into the New Testament picture more and more.

But Paul wrote "Paul and Timothy." Paul was probably dictating the letter to Timothy, his corresponding secretary.

Timothy's failure did not dislodge him from his place on Paul's team. By including Timothy at the beginning of the letter, Paul also reminded the Corinthians of this fact.

Soon Timothy and Paul would see the Corinthian Christians again; the two of them together would visit the site of their failure; and together they would build a church that would be strong and solid.

Why had Titus succeeded when Timothy failed? Perhaps Paul's letter C, with its strong admonition to the Corinthians, had helped effect a change in attitudes. Then too as William LaSor states: "Titus was probably somewhat older than Timothy and he had had a few more years' experience. Possibly he had certain personal qualifications that Timothy lacked, as for example, self-confidence or boldness. It is even possible that Timothy had, knowingly or unknowingly, prepared the way for Titus; the Corinthians had had time to regret how they had treated Timothy and may have determined to act toward Titus in a more Christian manner (*Great Personalities,* p. 153).

Failure and Success

When there is failure, it is good to examine the reasons for it, but it is even more important to determine what to do next.

In Timothy's case, it would take some forgiveness. When Paul put Timothy's name at the top of the Second Epistle to the Corinthians, it meant that Timothy had agreed to such phrases as "you have such a place in our hearts that we would live or die with you" (2 Cor. 7:13, NIV).

Failure is discouraging, but it is not necessarily final. We must go on. To Timothy that meant he had to go on to Corinth where he had been badly received the last time. To the student in school, it may mean repeating an entire grade. To an athlete who has been booed by thousands of fans for striking out with the bases loaded, it means going out of the dugout again and facing the same pitcher and possibly striking out again.

Timothy's hallmark, however, had never been success; it had been faithfulness. God hadn't promised him a gold medal; He had simply asked him to be faithful.

In our day, too many Christians are afraid of failure. As a result, little is ventured. Success has become a god, and we want to be successful in everything we do, from business to sex. As a result, we seek to cover up failures; we think it is disgraceful not to be successful at everything we attempt. Our lives become dishonest as we try to project a totally successful image.

One of the delightful expressions of our day is "I goofed." The people whom God uses are never goof-proof.

Jesus once told a story about a man with three servants. To each of them he gave a share of his wealth. To one, he gave five talents; to another, he gave two talents; to a third, he gave one talent.

You know the parable. The men with five talents and with two talents were not afraid to fail. The man who had been given only one talent did nothing with it. He said, "I was afraid, and went and hid thy talent in the earth" (Matt. 25:25).

In his book *The Fear of Failure,* G. Don Gilmore says, "What we need today is not another philosophy on how to succeed, but rather one on how to fail creatively" (Revell). Great men are made by their failures more often than by their successes.

Abraham Lincoln is perhaps the best-known example. He was a failure in business; he was a failure as a lawyer; he failed to become a candidate for the state legislature. He was thwarted in his attempt to become commissioner of the General Land Office. He was defeated in his bids for the vice-presidency and the Senate. But he didn't let failure ruin his life. Nor did he allow failure to embitter him toward people.

Looking at it one way, even Jesus Christ seemed to fail. "He came unto His own, and His own received Him not"! (John 1:11). As Gilmore puts it: "His family did not understand Him; the religious authorities hated Him; the political leadership was opposed to Him; His friends deserted Him; a disciple betrayed Him; vocal supporters denied Him; His congregation spit on Him—hurled stones at Him; His enemies crucified Him. He died on an ignominious cross, and it seemed even that God had forsaken Him." What an apparent failure!

But He is the One through whom we are more than conquerors. He is the One who has been exalted to the highest place and given a name which is above every name. He is the One who always causes us to triumph.

Our acquaintance with Jesus Christ helps us put life into perspective. It helps us see that failures are always short-term. Granted, Timothy had failed on a short-term assignment, but he had been faithful; and that faithfulness insured long-term success.

Life would have been a lot easier if Paul and Timothy had not begun preaching and teaching in Corinth. Anyone could see when they stepped into Corinth, that the town was filled with trouble. Any church founded there was sure to bring heartaches and grief continually.

And to send young Timothy back to Corinth was foolishness. Failure was guaranteed. It was Mission Impossible. It would bring him much anguish of soul.

Then why did Paul attempt to win Corinth for Christ? Because the Lord put it on his heart.

But if He put it on Paul's heart, why didn't He make success easier? Why were there so many failures along the way? Why were Paul and Timothy so "pressed out of shape," or, as Paul expressed it to the Corinthians, "pressed out of measure"? (2 Cor. 1:8)

An anonymous poem may give a few answers:

Pressed out of measure and pressed to all length,
Pressed so intently, it seems beyond strength,
Pressed in the body, and pressed in the soul,
Pressed in the mind till the dark surges roll,
Pressure by foes and pressure by friends,
Pressure on pressure till life nearly ends.

Pressed into knowing no helper but God,
Pressed into loving the staff and the rod,
Pressed into liberty where nothing clings,
Pressed into faith for impossible things,
Pressed into living a life for the Lord,
Pressed into living a Christ-life outpoured.

That's why, Timothy.

8

The Meaning of the Red Letters

As I was growing up, I owned a red-letter edition of the Bible, and I noticed that there were some red letters where I didn't expect them.

Since the red letters indicated the words of Christ, I found most of them in the Gospels and a few in the first chapter of Acts before His ascension, and still more in the Book of Revelation, recording Jesus' words to John the Beloved in his memorable vision.

But in the 148 chapters of the New Testament between Acts 1 and Revelation, there weren't very many red letters.

One exception, however, was Acts 20:35: "It is more blessed to give than to receive."

I used to wonder about those red letters buried in Acts. Why were they there?

When we left Paul and Timothy at the end of the last chapter, they were somewhere on the Egnatian Road, part of Rome's Route 66. Even as he wrote Corinthians D (what we call 2 Corinthians), Paul had his eyes focused westward, far down the Egnatian Highway to

Rome, the capital of the world, and beyond that to the far country of Spain on the western edge of the Mediterranean.

And when the Apostle Paul determined to go somewhere, it was pretty hard to change his mind.

In fact, after getting Titus' favorable report about the Corinthian church, and probably after writing 2 Corinthians from Philippi (or Thessalonica), Paul and Timothy trekked westward on the Egnatian Expressway about 200 miles to Illyricum, the westernmost province of Greece that faced Italy across the Adriatic Sea. From there, Paul could almost smell Rome.

After preaching awhile in Illyricum, Paul and Timothy went down to Corinth, spending about three months there.

One would naturally assume that Paul would devote all his time in Corinth to preaching and putting out congregational fires. After all, the church there seemed to be a victim of Murphy's famous law: "If something can possibly go wrong, it will." But Paul did have time for one extracurricular activity in Corinth: He wrote the Epistle to the Romans, with its systematic presentation of the great doctrines of Christianity.

Though Paul had never been to Rome, he knew a lot about it. Priscilla and Aquila, whom he had first met at the tentmakers' quarters in Corinth, and who later had helped him in Ephesus, were now back at their business headquarters in Rome. (Old Emperor Claudius had just died, so it was safe to return.) Priscilla and Aquila no doubt had whetted Paul's appetite to visit the church in the capital city, although I doubt if Paul's appetite needed much whetting.

However, his real goal was Spain, not Rome, as he plainly told the Roman Christians in his letter: "I have been longing for many years to see you. I plan to do so when I go to Spain. I hope to visit you while passing through and to have you assist me on my journey there, after I have enjoyed your company for a while'' (Rom. 15:23-24, NIV).

Who knows where else Paul was thinking of going? Maybe to Gaul; maybe even to that island outpost in the far northwest—Brittania.

So what was keeping him? Why wasn't he checking the timetables of all boats headed west? Because he had reservations on a ship headed east. East? Yes, there was something more important at the moment than preaching and teaching the Gospel in Rome. Timothy had known about it for the past three years. He knew that there was nothing that could deter Paul from his pet project.

It was more than a pet project; it was actually a grand operation. It would involve all the churches that Paul had founded to date. Each one would contribute to a massive relief fund to be taken to the poverty-stricken members of the church of Jerusalem.

Financial Need in Rome

Paul's concern went back 10 years or more to the time when the Christian church in Antioch undertook a famine relief program for the Jerusalem church. Paul and Barnabas had been designated as the couriers by the church in Antioch to take the money to their "brothers living in Judea" (Acts 11:29, NIV).

When misunderstandings later arose with the Jerusalem church, Peter, James, and John suggested to Paul that the best thing they could do would be to "continue to remember the poor," which Paul says was "the very thing I was eager to do" (Gal. 2:10, NIV).

On his most recent trip to Jerusalem, Paul must have been struck again by the great financial needs of the people. Hardly anything is reported in the New Testament about this visit, but from then on Paul started talking about a special relief drive for the Christians in Jerusalem.

When we read the Gospels, we tend to think of the people in Bible times as having the same standard of living that we are accustomed to today. But such was not the case, as Henri Daniel Rops points out in *Daily Life in the Times of Jesus:* "One should never forget that in Israel at that period, there existed a proletariat and even a class below that, made up of ill-paid workers (one denarius a day; four or five at the very most), day laborers with unemployment hanging over their heads . . . freedmen whose masters would not always give them that little sum that the Law desired them to give, beggars poverty-stricken in the streets, and, it must be remembered, lepers and cripples for whom there was no hospital. It was among these despised people, these outcasts, that Christ's message first spread, and that it went on spreading" (Hawthorn, p. 158).

That's a description of normal times. What must life have been like in the midst of a severe economic depression? As Rops says, "The economic crisis of the first century made the misery even worse."

When Paul had arrived in Jerusalem after spending two years in the prosperous cities of Corinth and Ephesus, he must have been shocked at the contrast.

Immediately, the gigantic plan emerged. When Paul came through Galatia in A.D. 52, picking up Timothy along the way, he told the Galatians about it and probably said that Timothy would come back in a year and pick up an offering from them. When Paul wrote his first letter to the church in Corinth, he said, "Do what I told the Galatian churches to do" (1 Cor. 16:1, NIV). When Paul wrote to the Romans (who weren't a part of the grand scheme, because they weren't one of the churches

Paul had launched), he explained the collection to them: "They (the new churches) have an obligation to help the poor. The Jews shared their spiritual blessings with the Gentiles, and so the Gentiles ought to serve the Jews with their material blessings." (See Rom. 15.27.)

No question about it; the subject was continually on Paul's mind.

Why Take an Offering, Paul?

If I had been Timothy, I would have had some questions for Paul when the subject first came up:

1. "Why get bogged down with gathering a collection, when there are so many other more important things to do—such as winning souls for Christ?

2. "Why upset new Christians? There is nothing that riles people more than asking for an offering. These new churches are already beset by so many problems; why add another one?

3. "Most of the new Christians are straddling the poverty line themselves. Isn't it a bit unfair to burden them down with an appeal to give to other poverty-stricken people? Or maybe you could exempt from giving those whose income level is no more than two denarii a day.

4. "If you're going to insist on passing the collection plate, Paul, why not think up another appeal? There are all sorts of reasons why giving to Jerusalem doesn't make sense:

● "Ever since you were converted, Paul, the Jerusalem church has given you a hard time. If they have problems now, maybe they deserve them. Maybe God is punishing the church for the way they have mistreated you. What did they ever give you but a peck of trouble?

● "If you're collecting an offering, why don't you use it to pay your way to Spain? You could start a mission called "End of the World Mission Society" and get enough money to underwrite a full term of missionary service in Spain for both you and myself.

● "Wouldn't it be more popular (and in the long run more lucrative) if you encouraged each church to start a building fund so each one could have a worshipful place to come and hear God's Word?"

This Is Why, Timothy

Paul had taught Timothy a lot about setting priorities, about organization, and about strategy during the past six or seven years that the two had been together. But never were all these matters combined more effectively than in the collection of the offering for the needy saints at Jerusalem.

The collection was not only an act of compassion and charity; it was also a teaching tool. Let's go back to those hypothetical questions for a minute and see how Paul might have answered them.

1. "My top priority is not the saving of souls, but the establishing of churches. If I were merely interested in soul-winning, I would not have written any epistles.

2. "One of the main things that new Christians need to understand is that they are part of a body composed of many members, and these members should love and care for each other. This body is most clearly visible in the local church; that's why I was so upset about how the Corinthians were tearing apart the body. But secondly, this body is also seen in the unity of all believers wherever they are. Remember these two things always: The church is the body of Christ, and it is *one* body.

3. "You said that these new Christians aren't rich. True, but don't forget that the first one who is blessed by a gift is the donor, not the receiver. The motivation for giving is not because you have and you ought, but be-

cause someone else has not and you love.

4. "Yes, I know that it hasn't been easy to deal with the Jerusalem church, but these Christians also need to know the truth of the body of Christ. They need to know that they are in the same body as the Corinthians, for example, and that there is a bond that unites us, whether we be Jew or Gentile, slave or free, male or female, black or white, rich or poor, brilliant or dull.

● "You say that the Jerusalem church doesn't deserve a ift. Maybe they don't, but don't you see that this is what Christianity is all about? God sent His Son not because we deserved Him, but because He loves us. If God had given us our just deserts, He would have zapped us long ago.

● "Just before He went into the Garden of Gethsemane, Jesus told His disciples several times to love one another. He said, 'By this shall all men know that ye are My disciples, if ye have love one to one another' (John 13:35). We must demonstrate that love.

● "So you see, there's nothing more important in the advancement of God's work than the displaying of Christian love between the churches—not even the preaching of the Gospel in far-off Spain.

● "As for the need to build churches, this would only make these young Christians become more focused upon themselves. Right now they are too concerned about their own petty problems. They need to think of something bigger, something beyond themselves. They need to start thinking about the needs of others.

"You question whether the Jerusalem Relief Fund is the right thing to do at this time. The more I think about it, the more I'm convinced it is not only the right thing to do, but it deserves top priority."

Well, I don't know how much of that Paul would actually have said to Timothy, but if you read 2 Corinthians 8 and 9, you will find many of those same arguments in Paul's own words.

Apologetic for Giving

Earlier, when Paul wrote his first letter to the church of Corinth, he started the ball rolling. He told them that giving should be regular, "upon the first day of the week" as a part of their worship; it should be proportionate, "as God hath prospered him"; and it should apply to all, "every one of you" whether rich or poor (1 Cor. 16:2).

In the following 12 months, the Corinthian Christians had a few other problems on their minds, so when Paul wrote his second epistle, he had to prod them a bit: "Now finish the work" (2 Cor. 8:11, NIV).

Earlier, no doubt, he had spelled out the desperate need of the Jerusalem Christians; now he followed it up with four more reasons: (1) The poor churches in Macedonia have already given; they have given out of poverty; shouldn't you be willing to give out of your affluence? (8:1-5) (2) As a church you possess many spiritual gifts; why don't you also cultivate the gift of giving? (8:6-7) Shortly afterward, in writing to the Romans, Paul listed *giving* as one of the gifts of the Spirit. (See Rom. 12:6-8.) (3) There is no greater example of giving than the example of Jesus Christ. Since He gave everything for you, why do you withhold from your brother? (8:8-9) This was the supreme argument. James Stewart has referred to it as "using a sledgehammer to crack a nut." (4) Giving is a means of evening things out; if you as the members of the Christian church learn to love one another, then sometime in the future when economic depression strikes Corinth, you will receive help from others (8:13-16).

Organization Is Necessary

Paul could make a convincing case. But Timothy learned a lot more than a few arguments for giving during the Jerusalem relief operation. He learned something about organization.

Sometimes you hear people say that if you are truly spiritual, you don't need organization. They imply that organization is a hindrance to the work of the Spirit.

I have to admit that sometimes that's true. It's possible for churches and Christian organizations to get so wrapped up in bureaucratic red tape that *Roberts Rules of Order* becomes more authoritative than the Bible, and prayer meetings are replaced by committee meetings.

But the Apostle Paul had a high regard for organization. And if Timothy was going to follow in Paul's footsteps, he had better learn how to organize things too.

Whenever a church was established, Paul always saw to it that it was properly organized. Timothy knew that from firsthand experience. And if you want to talk about truly effective organization, you should look at the Jerusalem Relief Fund.

In our day people have become accustomed to giving. In Paul's day, however, there was no Red Cross or United Fund. Plenty of beggars sat at the city gates, but that was about the extent of training anyone received in voluntary giving.

If you were going to raise funds from 8 or 10 churches scattered over several provinces and located up to 1,000 miles apart, how would you do it?

Well, here's how Paul did it. About a year in advance of Donation Day, each church was notified about the project, and given the opportunity to name a delegate (or approve of Paul's appointee) to carry its offering to Jerusalem. In some cases, Paul wrote follow-up letters and dispatched personal messengers to check up on the progress of the various churches. All the delegates were apparently told to meet in Corinth on a specified day, probably early in March, A.D. 57.

Everything was arranged with the precision of a 20th-century business operation.

For the Feast of Pentecost

Why was the date so important? That was part of Paul's plan too. He wanted to arrive in Jerusalem for the feast of Pentecost, which was in late May that year.

What was so important about the feast of Pentecost? Pentecost was a time of joy when all Jews were supposed to come to Jerusalem bringing the firstfruits of the fields and orchards from the spring harvest as an offering to the Lord. It was sort of a Jewish thanksgiving.

Of course, Christians today recognize Pentecost as the birthday of the Christian church (Acts 2:1), but Paul no doubt had the Old Testament meaning in mind. When he came to Jerusalem, he would be bringing the firstfruits of his ministry among the Gentiles and each one of them would be carrying an offering.

The Gentiles in his troupe of delegates probably didn't understand the significance and the symbolism of all of this, but you can be sure that Timothy did. Perhaps Paul and Timothy even envisioned this as the firstfruits of the fulfillment of prophecies such as: "In the lead are the ships of Tarshish, bringing your sons from afar, with their silver and gold, to the honor of the Lord your God, the Holy One of Israel" (Isa. 60:9, NIV).

Timothy was involved in the fund-raising process in several places. As a delegate of the church of Lystra, he was present when Paul first presented the appeal to the church there, and no doubt a year or two later, he returned to receive the funds that had been collected in his home church.

Later, Timothy was sent along with Erastus to Macedonia (Acts 19:22), and part of their purpose must have been to make sure that the fund-raising drive was on schedule in Philippi and Thessalonica. If this Erastus was indeed the Erastus who later became the Corinthian city treasurer (Rom. 16:23), he would have been a most trustworthy companion for Timothy in this fund-raising mission.

Despite all of Paul's detailed plans, he feared there might be problems. Probably in February A.D. 57, he wrote his letter to the Romans in which he begged the Christians there to pray for him. "I urge you . . . to join me in my struggle by praying to God for me" (Rom. 15:30, NIV). In March when he and his group of six or eight delegates were about to sail for Jerusalem, he discovered there was a plot against his life. On board a crowded ship, Paul would have been an easy target. So he suddenly changed his travel plans. Most of the delegates took the boat to the first stop along the way, the port of Troas; Paul, Luke, and maybe Titus went by land to Philippi and then took a short boat ride to meet the others at Troas. Fortunately, Paul had allowed enough leeway in his schedule for such minor problems as plots against his life.

A Stop at Ephesus

The next stop was down the Aegean coast, near Ephesus, and Paul couldn't pass up the opportunity to summon the elders of the Ephesian church to meet with him. In a moving sermon, he told them, "Now compelled by the Spirit, I am going to Jerusalem, not knowing what will happen to me there. I only know that in every city the Holy Spirit warns me that prison and hardships are facing me." And then he added, "None of you will ever see me again." (See Acts 20:38.)

You can be sure there wasn't a dry eye in the place. But the unasked question was, "If you know 'prison and hardship' await you in Jerusalem, why do you insist on going?"

Almost sensing a question like that, Paul concluded his talk to the Ephesian elders by quoting the words of Jesus, "'It is more blessed to give than to receive'" (Acts 20:35). (Remember the red letters I wondered about as a young person?)

Some of the modern translations put it this way: "It is happier to give than to receive."

Happier, Paul? You're on your way to present a gift to Christians in Jerusalem, knowing full well that prison and hardship await you. Does that bring you happiness, Paul?

Well, it isn't the superficial kind of happiness that comes from entertainment or from enjoying the good life. It's more like the happiness that Christ spoke about in what we call the Beatitudes: "Blessed are the meek, Blessed are they that mourn, Blessed are they that do hunger and thirst after righteousness." (See Matt. 5.)

It's the deeper happiness, a happiness that a sincere disciple like Timothy would need to learn more about.

After Paul finished speaking, "they all wept sore" (Acts 20:37), and you can be sure that Paul's companions on the Jerusalem trip did their share of weeping too.

On the Way to Jerusalem

You would think at this point that Timothy or one of the other delegates would have said, "Paul, if the Holy Spirit is telling you about the dangers ahead, why do you still persist in going?" They knew what his answer would have been: "It is by the same Holy Spirit that I am compelled to go."

It would have been easier to go west to Rome instead

of east to Jerusalem, and much safer. And there was still time to cancel his reservation to Jerusalem. But to Paul, the delivery of the collection to help the poor in Jerusalem was of utmost importance. As he told the Ephesian elders, "I consider my life worth nothing to me, if only I may finish the race and complete the task the Lord Jesus has given me' (Acts 20:24, NIV).

I am not surprised that Paul continued his voyage to Jerusalem. What surprises me is that none of the delegates defected. It would have been an appropriate time for one of them to develop some psychosomatic ailment. After all, Timothy did have a weak stomach.

When they all arrived in Palestine about a week later, they received another ominous warning. In the city of Tyre, Christians warned Paul not to go to Jerusalem. Their entreaties didn't seem to faze Paul. It was still early in May, so Paul and his team rested there for a week before continuing. Two days later they stopped at Caesarea, only 60 miles from Jerusalem. There they were met by a prophet who had come directly from Judea. Dramatically, the prophet took Paul's belt and wrapped it around his own hands and feet, saying, "This is what's going to happen to you if you go any further." (See Acts 21:10-11.)

Paul had to be shaken by this warning. You see, 10 or 12 years earlier, this same prophet had predicted a famine in Judea (Acts 11:28). It was his prophecy which prompted the church in Antioch to collect the first Jerusalem Famine Relief Fund. And now, after all these years, he appeared again, as Paul was about to deliver another relief fund.

For Timothy and the other delegates, this was the last straw. Maybe Paul had made a mistake after all, they reasoned. Maybe God really didn't want him to go to Jerusalem. Perhaps Paul could stay behind while the delegates went ahead to present the offering to the church leaders in Jerusalem. Most of them were unknown in Jerusalem. If Jerusalem had had post offices, Paul's picture would have been plastered on the walls as the "Most Wanted Man."

So together with the Caesarean Christians—and this would have included Philip the evangelist and his four daughters, all of whom were prophets—the delegates begged Paul not to be so stubborn. Couldn't he see that the Holy Spirit was telling him not to go any farther? Even Timothy disagreed with Paul's decision to go to Jerusalem.

When even his closest friends begged him to change his course, Paul had to respond. How did he answer them? "Why all these tears? Why are you trying to weaken my resolution? For my part I am ready not merely to be bound but even to die at Jerusalem for the name of the Lord Jesus." (See Acts 21:13.)

Paul was determined. He knew what awaited him, but he could not be dissuaded from continuing. Perhaps he had some of the same feelings that Jesus had when He took that last long walk from Galilee to Jerusalem, knowing that the cross of Calvary awaited Him.

The discussion was concluded by a very revealing statement: "And when he would not be persuaded, we ceased, saying, 'The will of the Lord be done'" (Acts 21:14).

I don't know if you've ever come to times in your life like that, but I have. Perhaps you feel strongly one way; a friend or loved one feels strongly another way. You feel that God is directing in one way; your friend feels that God is urging another way. You feel that all the arguments are on your side, but your friend will not be persuaded.

You're disappointed; of course you are. Your friend

won't listen to reason. You're discouraged because your advice was given for the good of your friend and he decided to disregard it. If your motives were wrong, it would be different. But you prayed about it and you did it for your friend's good, not your own. You're distraught because your friend is determined, against your wise counsel, to walk straight into trouble. You feel sad for him and for what he will undoubtedly face.

That's the way Timothy, Luke, and the others must have felt.

There are a few commentators who feel that after discussing the matter with Paul, Timothy, Luke, and the other delegates realized that their mentor was in God's will, and they weren't. But I don't think so.

At this point, I don't think they knew what the will of the Lord was. It seemed to them that Paul should stay at Caesarea, but Paul was sure that God wanted him to continue, so they said, "The will of the Lord be done," and they went with him.

That wasn't easy.

One wise old 19th-century preacher (J.C. Vaughan) wrote, "It is a hard thing to sit and watch one I love and to school my heart to receive I do not know what, and I am afraid to ask what. But all the while, far above all this, over the perplexity and over the mystery and over the dread, there is reigning the high will of God, and that will is bearing on to its own destined purpose, and it must prevail. And here is faith's large field—the unrevealed will of God."

What God had revealed to Paul was not revealed to Timothy. This didn't mean that Timothy was any less spiritual at this point than Paul. It merely meant that Timothy had to say, "I don't understand it, Lord; it doesn't make sense to me, but may Your will be done."

And that may have been as hard to do as it was for

Paul to take the road God had chosen for him.

Then the men began their trek up to Jerusalem. The trip from Caesarea to Jerusalem was 60 miles, all uphill, for Jerusalem is perched on hills a half mile above sea level. It is possible that horses were provided for the last lap of their long journey, at least to carry their baggage.

It's what Jewish pilgrims called "climbing the ascent." We sing the hymn, "We're Marching to Zion," with a carefree lilt. But Timothy, Luke, and the others had no carefree feeling on their march to Zion.

Imagine what it must have been like for Timothy. Probably, this was the first visit he had made to Jerusalem. He had dreamed about this day all his life, as any Jewish lad would have. When Paul had first mentioned the Jerusalem relief fund to him, Timothy must have been excited about the possibility of being a delegate. When he was approved by the Lystran church as its delegate, he realized that his lifetime dream would soon become true. But now the joy had gone out of it.

As he and the other delegates caught their first glimpse of Jerusalem in the distance, they knew it was customary for pilgrims to sing one of the Psalms of Ascent. A series of psalms was written for such a purpose, psalms that begin like this one: "I was glad when they said unto me, 'Let us go into the house of the Lord'" (Ps. 122:1). But other psalms seemed more appropriate now, such as "Those who sow in tears shall reap in joy," or "The Lord will watch over your going out and your coming in both now and forevermore." (See Pss. 126:5; 121:8.)

What lay ahead of them in Jerusalem? What was Paul's future? And what did the future hold for Timothy?

When they arrived in Jerusalem, they were greeted warmly by the Christian brethren; nothing sinister at all happened. But the delegates must have felt the uncertainty hanging heavily upon them. Something would be happening soon. They had committed themselves to God when they said, "The will of the Lord be done." But it would be only human to wonder what would be involved and in exactly what way it would be accomplished.

The day after arriving, Paul and his company went to meet James, the brother of Jesus, who was serving as the leader of the Jerusalem church. All the elders of the church were assembled there as well.

On this auspicious occasion, the delegates must have turned over the relief funds to the elders of the church and taken time to praise God. Paul gave a detailed report of all that God had done among the Gentiles through his ministry. The report probably continued for several hours.

Trouble in Jerusalem

So far, so good. But within a week everything had changed. Taking the advice of the Jerusalem elders, Paul had accompanied four local Christians who wished to fulfill a vow in the temple. The elders thought that Paul's presence in the temple might quash the rumor that Paul had forsaken his Jewish roots.

The plan backfired. Instead of placating the rumor-mongers, Paul's presence there gave birth to new rumors. According to the latest one, Paul was desecrating the temple by bringing Gentiles into it.

What happened thereafter was par for the course when Paul was around: a riot in the temple, a dramatic rescue by Roman soldiers, an assassination plot by 40 dagger-men, a 500-man military escort taking Paul by night to Roman headquarters in Caesarea.

The prophecies regarding trouble had come to pass. Prison and hardship for Paul seemed certain.

What about Timothy and the other delegates? In a strange city, buffeted by events that moved faster than they could keep up with, Timothy and the others must have been confused and bewildered.

Especially Timothy. For nearly eight years he had been Paul's right-hand man. He was 26 or 27 now, but had never been completely on his own. Even when he had been traveling on missions for Paul, he was under orders, and had faithfully carried his assignments out to the best of his ability. His latest task had been to escort the relief fund to Jerusalem, but now the job was finished. Timothy was unemployed.

Most of the other delegates probably had jobs to return to and no doubt looked for the next ship back home. They would report back to their respective churches that they had completed their missions, and they would request prayer for Paul who was incarcerated in a Roman prison in Caesarea.

But Timothy had been trained as a missionary. His experience had been chiefly in working with young churches.

Two of the delegates—Aristarchus, representing Thessalonica, and Dr. Luke, no doubt representing Philippi—stayed with Paul in Caesarea. Apparently, Aristarchus stayed as a personal servant and Luke as Paul's physician.

But what about Timothy? What would happen to him? And I wonder if Timothy understood the meaning of those red letters I saw years ago in Acts 20:35: "It is more blessed to give than to receive."

9

Timothy as Brother

It's too bad that they didn't have telephones in Paul's day; he wouldn't have had to write so many long letters. And think of how much of Timothy's time they would have saved; it took six weeks to go 1,000 miles.

But what a gigantic phone bill Paul would have had each month! He would have been on the phone constantly to Epaphroditus or Archippus or Titus or Aristarchus or one of those other church workers whose names are equally hard to pronounce.

Paul's concern for all those infant churches was like that of a mother whose four teenaged children are spending the summer in four different parts of the country. She would like to be in all four places at once. Nowhere is Paul's concern more clearly seen than when he was under house arrest in Rome in the years A.D. 60–62. But we're getting ahead of the story.

Paul, you remember, was put in prison in Caesarea. The story of how he appealed to Caesar (that's Nero, remember) for a fair trial is told dramatically in the Book of Acts. As a Roman citizen, he had that right; so after two years of confinement in Caesarea (Governor Felix was hoping for a little under-the-table money from Paul, so he wasn't in a hurry), Paul was shipped off to Rome. On the way, he endured a shipwreck, during which the records of his court case were probably lost at sea. He finally ended up in Rome in the spring of A.D. 60, and was promptly put under house arrest while waiting for trial.

Timothy stayed behind in Caesarea, but three years later he turned up in Rome. There's no record about his activities in the interim; all we can do is make calculated guesses.

Knowing Timothy, it's quite possible that he and perhaps another delegate, Tychicus, a native of Ephesus, stayed in Caesarea as long as they could. When they heard that Paul had appealed his case to Caesar in Rome, they knew that there was nothing more that could be done for him in Palestine. So my guess is that they took the land route to Rome, visiting the fledgling churches en route, and requesting prayer for Paul.

Luke and Aristarchus, you remember, stayed with Paul as personal servants and were allowed to take the ill-fated ship with Paul. Probably, Timothy would have liked to board the ship himself. But no one knew the churches better than he did, so it was natural that he would notify the concerned Christians of what was happening. It's quite possible that Paul himself dispatched Timothy and Tychicus on this mission.

If that scenario is right, Timothy and Tychicus would have visited the churches in Galatia, including Timothy's hometown of Lystra, where he could spend some time with his aging mother. They probably went on to Colossae, a church which Paul had not founded, but which Timothy had visited; then to Ephesus, the hometown of Tychicus, and on through Troas to Philippi, where they would have alerted the Christians about Paul's need for prayer. From Philippi, they may have followed the Egnatian Way, stopping, of course, at Thessalonica, and Berea, before crossing the Adriatic Sea and taking the Appian Way into Rome.

It's all conjecture, of course, but it does make sense. At any rate, we know from the epistles that Timothy and Tychicus, who were last seen and heard of in Jerusalem around A.D. 58, were in Rome around A.D. 61 along with Luke, Aristarchus, and, of course, Paul.

Timothy would have been about 30 years old and Paul about 60.

By this time, Timothy had become well acquainted with several big cities. Ephesus, Corinth, Thessalonica all were cities of 200,000 or more. But Rome was different. A city with a population of 1.2 million, about 400,000 of whom were slaves, and with a Jewish population of about 50,000 (there may have been nearly as many Jews in Rome as lived in Jerusalem), Rome had many of the same complex urban problems we have today. Its biggest problem was pollution; urban housing was another. It had high-rise apartments (if you call six-stories a high-rise), and a full assortment of athletic events and entertainment to amuse the citizenry. Besides all of that, it was rapidly developing into a welfare state.

Paul as a Prisoner

So Rome was a rather unique city in its day. And Paul was a rather unique prisoner. He was not chained in a little cubbyhole at this time (that comes later), but he had his own house, which he rented. However, he was under constant guard by the emperor's select troops. Many of Paul's friends came to Rome for one reason or another, and there seemed to be a steady flow of visitors coming to the house.

But it was a nuisance to be chained to a soldier, and for Paul, who had so many things he wanted to do and places he wanted to visit, it was a hardship to be confined to a house. He was impatient to appear before Nero.

But one of three things may have happened which delayed Paul's court case: (1) Since the records of the case were probably lost at sea, the officials may have had to write back to Caesarea to have new records prepared; (2) the docket may have been filled with other cases which had to be heard first; or (3) they may have been waiting for the prosecution (the Jewish leaders from Jerusalem) to appear to present their case against Paul.

You would think that with Paul's relative freedom, he would have had a great time ministering to the Christians in Rome. But frankly, the Roman Christians were a disappointment to him.

Christianity had come to Rome by unknown Jewish converts nearly 30 years earlier, and had grown "like Topsy." It seemed to lack organization, something that Paul always insisted on in the churches which he established. There were many independent house churches in Rome. Some of them seemed to resent Paul's presence in their city; after all, certain ones may have existed before Paul had been converted. Others ignored him. Nero was starting to show his true colors and it seemed wise not to fraternize with people in prison. But there were still others who cared for Paul.

Although Paul's contacts with the Roman church were disappointingly sparse, his contacts with Nero's choicest soldiers were plentiful. There was always a soldier at the end of the chain.

William Barclay says, "What a chance was there! These soldiers would hear Paul preach and talk to his friends. Is there any doubt that in the long hours Paul would open up a discussion about Jesus with the soldier to whose wrist he was chained? Paul's imprisonment had opened the way for preaching the Gospel to the finest regiment in the Roman army, the Imperial Guards'' (*The Acts of the Apostles*, Westminster, p. 212).

The soldiers must have been impressed, not only by Paul's message, but also by his methods. They were accustomed to taking orders from their commanding officers, and it must have seemed that the Apostle Paul was a commanding officer in his own right. Timothy, Tychicus, Aristarchus, Luke, Mark, Epaphras, and others reported in to Paul's command headquarters, and then were dispatched on missions like soldiers, to do Paul's bidding hundreds of miles away. It was an efficient operation in military style.

It would seem that shortly after Timothy had arrived at Paul's prison headquarters, he was put to work. Perhaps because of problems with his eyes, Paul preferred not to write his own letters, and his assistants doubled as secretaries. Probably, Timothy had already served as Paul's secretary in the writing of 2 Corinthians; in Rome, Timothy apparently became the scribe to put into writing several other epistles.

Timothy's name is at the beginning of three epistles that Paul wrote from prison: Colossians, Philemon, and Philippians. This doesn't necessarily mean that he was the scribe, but many scholars feel that it is quite likely that he was. The only ''prison'' epistle that doesn't have Timothy's name attached to it is Ephesians, a letter with a different writing style, even though some of the content is similar to the Letter to the Colossians. Luke might have been the scribe for the Ephesian epistle before Timothy arrived in Rome.

Behind each of the letters associated with Timothy, there is a story.

Church of Colossae

Story 1. Colossae was a little town about 100 miles up-river from Ephesus. It was known for earthquakes and its wool and dye industry. It could very well have escaped notice by the New Testament writers except that its church had a problem. (Its name appears only once in the Bible: Col. 1:2.)

Epaphras, who was probably converted through Paul's ministry at Ephesus, was the church's founding father, though Timothy may have had a hand in it too.

When trouble started brewing in Colossae, Epaphras was the man in the middle. He tried to put a lid on it, but was apparently unsuccessful. Concerned and feeling unequipped to handle the eruption, he went to Paul for help.

(Speaking of eruptions, there was also an earthquake in Colossae about that time, which may have been another reason for Epaphras' journey to Rome.)

The Colossian church had concocted a strange heretical doctrine which combined a bit of Jewish legalism, Greek philosophical dualism, and the Ephesian occult. It was a mixed-up mess.

Though the church was small and though Paul himself hadn't started it, he carried a deep concern for its welfare. So under the inspiration of the Holy Spirit, he wrote a warm but deeply profound epistle to the group there.

This is the way he began: "Paul, an apostle of Jesus Christ by the will of God, and Timothy our brother" (Col. 1:1, NASB).

Timothy was called many things by the Apostle Paul: his son, his fellow worker, a servant, a disciple, but most often he was called a brother.

And the reason why he was most often called a brother is that that's the way the churches regarded him. He had developed a fraternal relationship with those churches that was impossible for Paul to attain. Paul was the apostle, the authority figure. He was the father figure; Timothy was the brother figure, the one who stood side by side with them. Paul seemed to have all the answers; Timothy worked with them to find solutions. While the Colossians knew of Paul by reputation, it would seem that by the appellation *brother,* they somehow knew Timothy from firsthand experience.

Barclay says, "The first necessity for Christian service is the ability to 'get alongside' all kinds of people. Timothy is not described as the preacher, the teacher, the theologian, the administrator, but as the brother. He who walks in aloofness can never be a real servant of Jesus Christ" (*Philippians, Colossians, and Thessalonians,* Westminster, p. 124).

Brothers are sorely needed today. You often hear that the church needs more missionaries, pastors, teachers, and other workers. But in this day of loneliness and friendlessness, one of the biggest needs is for more brothers.

Paul addressed the Colossians as brothers and saints. As saints, they were special people, selected and set apart by God. They may have felt insignificant as citizens of Colossae, one of the tri-cities (Laodicea, Hierapolis, and Colossae), and always mentioned last. If Colossae had had a sports team, it would always have been in last place. But to God, Paul told the Colossian Christians, they were on the All-Star team.

Besides being saints, they were brothers: brothers to Brother Timothy, brothers to one another, and they were also brothers to all Christians scattered throughout the Roman Empire. They may have felt isolated in the backwaters of the Lycus Valley, but Paul said they were members of God's family, a family that wasn't provincial, a family that transcended national boundaries.

Yes, they were in Colossae, but they were also in Christ. They were brothers, but they were also saints.

Philemon

The church of Colossae met in the home of a well-to-do parishioner Philemon, a man about Paul's age. His slave Onesimus had run away to Rome and somehow had found Paul, no one knows how.

Regardless, Onesimus, whose name literally means "profitable or useful," soon became a Christian and also a useful and profitable servant for Paul. As Onesimus learned more and more of the Christian faith, Paul benefited from his services.

Hence a dilemma. Paul's cohorts were shuffling in and out of the Roman command post. It would be helpful to have someone permanently at Paul's side. But as a slave, Onesimus still belonged to Philemon back in Colossae; and Philemon was a leader in the Colossian church.

In our day, we would solve the problem rationally by saying that since slavery is wrong, Onesimus could stay in Rome. But in Paul's day, it wasn't that simple: Paul had to consider Philemon and what was best for him, and he had to consider Onesimus, and what was best for him.

So Paul did what he had to do. He asked Timothy to get out the quill and ink again, and he dictated a little note to his friend Philemon.

It's only 25 verses long, but it is one of the warmest letters in the New Testament. As you read it, you can have no doubt that Paul cared intensely for the welfare of both Philemon and Onesimus.

But what about slavery? How could Paul ignore the evils of slavery?

Take note how Paul wrote. He began by referring to himself, not as an apostle as he did to the entire Colossian church, but as a prisoner, which was the position that a runaway slave ought to assume. Timothy was also mentioned in the salutation. He was still called *brother,* but here the word has a special meaning.

Paul inserted the word *brother* when referring to Philemon, as well. In fact, he called him "his beloved brother."

Now legally, Philemon could do anything he wanted to with a runaway slave. He could even have Onesimus killed. In that society, slaves were nonpersons.

Paul knew that. You can be sure that Onesimus knew it too. So Paul asked Philemon for a little favor: to receive Onesimus back as a servant and as a beloved brother.

By the time Paul had finished dictating the letter, he had called Timothy a brother, Philemon a beloved brother, and also the slave Onesimus a beloved brother.

Sounds like one big happy family, doesn't it?

And it's very hard for slavery to exist within a happy family, isn't it?

You remember that when the Prodigal Son returned to his father, he asked to be brought back into the house as a slave. Instead, the father killed a fatted calf and put a ring on the son's finger.

As Timothy wrote the letter, he may have thought of the way his own life had been transformed. Timothy couldn't boast of spectacular gifts. He was not what you would call a "high-profit" servant. But when he became a son of God through faith in Jesus Christ, everything changed. He found himself part of a vast and growing brotherhood. He, like Onesimus, had been transformed into a beloved brother.

When Paul finished dictating those two epistles, he called Tychicus, asking him to accompany Onesimus and the two letters back to Colossae. The Ephesian letter (which may have been a circular letter addressed to the other churches in the area as well as to Ephesus) was carried by Tychicus at the same time.

Church at Philippi

Although living in his own rented quarters was far better than living in a Roman prison, it certainly cost a lot more. And it was impossible for Paul to make a living by making tents with a Roman soldier chained to his arm. Hence, he may have had some financial problems.

Then Epaphroditus walked in. He hardly looked like the man whom Paul and Timothy had known as a minister in Philippi. Obviously, Epaphroditus was very sick. Perhaps he had picked up the malarial bug in the swampy area south of Rome.

With Epaphroditus came a gift; the Christians in Philippi seemed to have a penchant for taking offerings. They had sent Paul at least one love offering while he was at Thessalonica and another one while he was in Corinth. They had also participated in the relief fund for the Christians in Jerusalem, and now once again they gave to meet Paul's personal needs. He was overwhelmed with gratitude.

Over the next several weeks, Epaphroditus was nursed back to health again and Paul's workers were dispatched to various locations. Probably Luke and Aristarchus, who had stayed with Paul through the shipwreck and his imprisonments in Caesarea and now in Rome, were also given assignments. But Timothy remained with Paul as the wait for his court case to come to trial stretched longer and longer.

Paul called Timothy to help him with another letter, this time to thank the Philippians for their generous gift, and to let them know how Epaphroditus was faring. It was a letter to share with them his personal feelings, and to straighten out a few minor problems and point to some danger signals which he had noted in the church of Philippi. Compared to the second Letter to the Corinthians, this was an easy letter to write.

I can imagine how Paul's mind may have gone back 12 years to his first days in Philippi with Silas and Timothy. He would have recalled Lydia, the businesswoman who had been the first convert, and the demon-possessed girl who had kept following them around shouting, "These men are slaves of the most high God."

That was it. That was the way that he would begin this epistle. Writing to other churches, Paul often had to remind them that he was an apostle, writing with authority. To the Philippians, proud of their citizenship in a Roman colony and proud of their heritage in the historic city, it seemed appropriate for him to begin, "Paul and Timothy, slaves of Jesus Christ." (See Phil. 1:1.)

Nothing else. Just slaves. That was the title Paul and Timothy had received from the demoniac slave girl. That was the day they had made the headlines, a day that the Philippian Christians would never forget.

Paul and Timothy rejoiced in the way the Philippian Christians had become partners in the Gospel "from the first day until now" (Phil. 1:5). The Philippian Christians were not content to be converts; they had become partners from the day that Lydia had opened her home to the four missionaries. Lydia's openheartedness had set a pattern that the Philippian Christians continued to emulate. They had a reputation of giving frequently and generously to the ministry of Paul and Timothy (Phil. 4:14-19). But their generosity was more than do-goodism. They felt themselves to be true partners, yokefellows (fellow slaves) in Paul's ministry. As a result, they were praying for him.

Paul no doubt recalled the time in the Philippian jail

when he and Silas had been praying on the inside and Timothy and the new Christians in Lydia's house had been praying on the outside. God had worked through an earthquake to accomplish His purpose that time. A jailer was saved and then his household, adding to the infant church in Philippi.

Now Paul was in prison again, and again his jailers were being saved (Phil. 1:12-13), and God was accomplishing His purposes for the good of the church (Phil. 1:14). Once again Paul was rejoicing (Phil. 1:18). Once again the Philippian Christians were praying on the outside, though 1,000 miles away, and Paul was praying on the inside (Phil. 1:19). With Christians like that in partnership with him, no wonder Paul could be confident that God would once again work all things together for good.

The progress report that their pastor Epaphroditus had brought to Rome was a good one. There was no need for a tongue-lashing. Yet there were some problems, such as the tendency toward pride.

The Philippian church needed models of humility.

Of course, the greatest Model of humility is Jesus Christ Himself, who left the glories of heaven to come to earth, who took the role of a slave (there's that word again), and died a criminal's death on the cross.

If Christians displayed such a humility in Philippi—or anywhere else—there would be no trouble with church splits. Humility is the resin, and love is the epoxy that cements a church together.

But what examples could Paul set before the Philippians? What models of humility could go to Philippi? Humility, after all, is a virtue that is understood better in the showing than in the telling.

What examples could Paul find? There was one seated in front of him. Timothy.

Timothy, one commentator says, "is the patron saint of all those who are quite content with the second place as long as they can serve."

British author Guy H. King tells a story about an Englishman who displayed the same quality. "When Sir Bartle Frere returned from India, the carriage was sent to the village station to bring him to his home. When the footman, newly engaged, asked how he should recognize Sir Bartle, his aged mother said, 'Look out for somebody helping someone else.'

"Sure enough, when the London train had drawn in, the manservant observed a gentleman assisting an old lady to the platform and then jumping back into the carriage to fetch out her luggage. Going straight up to him, the footman inquired, 'Sir Bartle?'

"Yes, it was he. What a lovely reputation to have. To be known as one who is always on the lookout to see when, and how, one can help others" (*First Timothy,* Christian Literature Crusade).

That was the kind of reputation Timothy had.

So Paul told the Philippians that he would soon be sending Timothy to visit them. Then he added, "For I have no man like-minded, who will naturally care for your state" (Phil. 2:20), or, as it says in the *New International Version,* "who takes a genuine interest in your welfare." Then Paul tacked on a sad sentence: "For everyone looks out for his own interests, not those of Jesus Christ" (Phil. 2:21, NIV).

One purpose of Timothy's promised visit was to bring the Philippians the latest news of the outcome of Paul's trial. But another purpose was to minister to them.

Paul says that Timothy was "like-minded," but with whom?

That question has had the commentators scratching their heads.

Of course, Timothy was like-minded with Paul. They had spent so much time together that Timothy was almost Paul's *alter ego*. Just as Paul was concerned about the Philippians, so was Timothy. "He therefore is a natural," says commentator William Hendriksen. "Yes, you can surely bank on it that he will be genuinely interested in your welfare" (*Philippians*, Baker, p. 134).

But besides that, Timothy had become like-minded with the Lord Jesus Christ. Paul had urged the Philippians to be like-minded with one another (Phil. 2:2) and also with the Lord, especially in regard to humility (2:5-8). Paul must have been thinking about the same idea when he used the word *like-minded* again a little later (2:20).

Actually, these references tell us three things about Timothy: He was concerned about Paul; he was concerned about the Philippians; and he was concerned about Jesus Christ.

That was a special combination that would unlock any situation. Paul knew it. In fact, when he wrote this epistle there was no one else around who possessed those three concerns. There were thousands of Christians in Rome by this time, but all of them seemed to be preoccupied with coping with the problems of daily life. Paul couldn't count on them for a mission like this.

Perhaps Paul would have preferred to keep Timothy with him and to send someone else. Evidently, he had even asked someone else to go, but his request had been met with excuses instead of with eagerness.

The bounty hunters of the Old West had the motto: "Have gun, will travel." Timothy's motto was, "Have concern, will travel."

That was Timothy's secret of success. He put the interests of Jesus Christ above his own interests. No wonder God found him so usable.

Timothy, as you are no doubt discovering by now, was quite an ordinary fellow. He did not possess extraordinary gifts nor did he exhibit remarkable courage.

He merely put the interests of Jesus Christ above his own interests.

Anyone can do that. But will he?

As soon as the epistle was finished, it was sent with Epaphroditus to Philippi. It is probable that Paul was released from prison in A.D. 62, and that immediately afterward Timothy went to Philippi to share the good news with the praying church.

"Father, where shall I work today?"
And my love flowed warm and free.
Then He pointed me out a tiny spot,
And said, "Tend that for Me."

I answered quickly, "Oh no, not that,
Why, no one would ever see,
No matter how well my work was done.
Not that little place for me!"

And the word He spoke, it was not stern,
He answered me tenderly,
"Ah, little one, search that heart of thine;
Art thou working for them or Me?
Nazareth was a little place,
And so was Galilee."

Author unknown

10

This Is Your Commander Speaking

Did you ever feel sorry for the outfielder who warmed the bench for years while Willie Mays was shagging flies for the Giants?

Or what about the second-string first baseman behind Lou Gehrig, the iron man of the Yankees, who played in every game for several years?

Year after year, they waited for their chance to play, waited for the golden opportunity to show that they were Major League caliber.

Have you ever felt like that? Have you ever wondered why God has given you some abilities that you have never had a chance to develop and display? Have you ever thought that if you had a chance to play regularly on the first team, you too could achieve stardom?

Not for Me

Well, for second-string Timothy, the chance of a lifetime had finally come. And he didn't want it.

For nearly 15 years Timothy had been coached by Paul, but he had never had a chance to carry the ball.

Now Paul was saying, "Timothy, I want you to stay in Ephesus and watch over the Christian church there."

This was quite a challenge. Ephesus was one of the five biggest cities in the Roman Empire. Since Paul and Timothy had started the first Christian church there (probably in the home of Priscilla and Aquila) about a dozen years earlier, scores of others had been started. House churches were sprouting up all over the place. It was exciting. It was also dangerous.

In Rome Paul had just witnessed the problems that can develop when there is a lack of organization. Somebody was needed in Ephesus to keep the churches from disintegrating the same way, somebody who had Paul's concern for organization, and who was not a dictator, somebody whom the Ephesians knew. Who else but Timothy?

Timothy must have felt something like a used car salesman being named president of the Ford Motor Company. He was in over his head again. He was wearing Paul's shoes, and they were size 13 EEE.

Besides, he was much better playing a second-fiddle role. He was certainly much more experienced in it. With his weak stomach and his timid disposition, how could he ever handle the church squabbles and doctrinal disputes that were inevitable in a parish the size of Ephesus?

The responsibility of the Ephesian churches would rest on his slender shoulders. Besides that, other churches in the area would be looking to Ephesus for leadership. Ephesus was the key city of Asia Minor.

Well, Timothy, what about it? As you read how Paul opened his letter to Timothy, you can guess what Timothy's natural inclinations were: "As I begged you to do when I was on my way to Macedonia, I still beg you to stay on in Ephesus" (1 Tim. 1:3, WMS). If Paul was begging Timothy to stay, it's obvious that Timothy would have preferred not to.

No, Timothy didn't want the job.

But it's even more obvious that Paul wanted him to take it. About 63 now, the aging apostle knew several things:

• Ephesus needed spiritual guidance as well as organization, and no one was better trained to give these things than Timothy.

• Timothy, about 33 years old, needed to be pushed out of the nest. The younger generation was going to have to take over Paul's responsibilities.

• Paul's days were numbered. He may still have had a missionary trip to Spain on his agenda, with perhaps a stop in Gaul on the way back; but realistically, a man in his 60s with sporadic health problems couldn't keep up a vigorous travel schedule for very many years. Besides, Emperor Nero was starting to kick up his heels. Now that he was no longer under the influence of Senators Burrus and Seneca who seemed to exercise some constraint on him, no one knew what Nero might do.

Timothy would just have to stay in Ephesus. There was no question about it. Paul had put his foot down and Timothy would have to do what he said.

You might wonder how Paul and Timothy got to Ephesus, when a year earlier they were in Rome, more than 1,000 miles to the west.

The Bible is virtually silent about their activities, but if we look closely we can spot a few clues.

As soon as Paul was released from prison in Rome (about A.D. 62), we can assume that he sent Timothy to Philippi as he had promised (Phil. 2:23). At the same time, Paul probably headed to Philemon's home in Colossae, also as he had promised (Phile. 22), perhaps stopping at Crete on the way (see Titus 1:5).

After a time of recuperation at Philemon's villa, Paul

headed back to Ephesus where Timothy joined him.

At this point, Timothy probably thought he would be Paul's traveling companion for a while. (Maybe even a trip to Spain's Costa del Sol was in the offing.) Instead, Timothy was placed in charge of the Ephesian sphere of influence while Paul went to visit the Macedonian churches. It was from Macedonia, shortly after Paul had left Timothy in Ephesus (perhaps about A.D. 63), that Paul's first epistle to Timothy was written.

Two Questions and Answers

Before we look at the contents of that letter, let's consider a couple of questions:

• Why would Paul write Timothy a letter? It may sound like a foolish question at first, but it isn't. You see, Paul and Timothy had just been together in Ephesus. No doubt they had discussed the problems of the Ephesian church over some Turkish coffee. Timothy was no stranger to Paul's thinking in regard to church administration or to church doctrine. If he didn't know Paul's thinking after 12 or more years of working with him, he was certainly a slow learner. Of all people, Timothy might be considered the least likely person to be the recipient of a letter at this time from the Apostle Paul.

• Why would Paul begin the letter the way he did? Listen to this salutation from a man who had worked side by side with Timothy: "Paul, an apostle of Jesus Christ by the commandment of God our Saviour, and Lord Jesus Christ, which is our hope" (1 Tim. 1:1).

That was like getting a letter from a sweetheart addressed to "To whom it may concern" and signed "Sincerely yours." It may be proper, but somehow you expect a bit more.

Paul usually referred to himself as an apostle when he was ready to lower the boom. When he wrote to the legalistic Galatians, the licentious Corinthians and the mixed-up Colossians, he needed to put some teeth into the words that followed. But when he wrote to Philemon, he referred to himself as a prisoner; when he wrote to the Philippians, he referred to himself as a slave or a servant.

So why did he call himself an apostle when writing to Timothy? Did he feel he had to impress Timothy with his authority?

My guess is that Paul had several good reasons for writing his letter to Timothy: (1) Obviously, he had to impress Timothy with the fact that he was needed more in Ephesus than he was with Paul. The situation in Ephesus was critical. (2) Paul thought he could give Timothy some personal encouragement, and in his situation, Timothy needed all the encouragement he could get. (3) While Paul and Timothy had no doubt discussed the Ephesian problems together, Paul felt it would be helpful to put things down in black and white. (4) Paul wanted to lend his apostolic authority to bolster Timothy in the big job he had ahead of him. And (5) in writing this epistle, Paul was providing an elementary church constitution for the mushrooming Ephesian church.

My answer to the second question is that Paul was not writing for Timothy alone. This letter would be shared with other leaders in the church who needed to know that the directions were backed by apostolic authority.

Timothy's Parish

Ephesus was caught in the crosscurrents of many Eastern and Western religions and philosophies. Since the city was located on the Pan-Asian highway, traveling teachers found it a convenient stopping place. As a result, the Ephesians heard a potpourri of zany cults and isms propounded.

In his Epistle to the Ephesians, written from Rome only a year or two earlier, Paul had warned the church about the danger of being "tossed to and fro, and carried about with every wind of doctrine" (Eph. 4:14).

That's why Paul had left Timothy at Ephesus. Timothy may not have looked like the Rock of Gibraltar; he may not have resembled a linebacker for the Dallas Cowboys; but when it came to doctrinal crosswinds, nothing could blow Timothy over.

Commentator William Hendriksen in his book, *First and Second Timothy and Titus* (Baker, p. 159), suggests that Timothy may have had the "gift of discernment" (see 1 Tim. 4:14). If he had, he certainly needed to exercise it now.

Timothy had his work cut out for him. If the Ephesian church kept the faith, it would be a model to all the others in the area. But if it fell—well, have you ever heard of the domino theory?

Humanly speaking then, the responsibility was Timothy's. Yet, as John Stott says, "Timothy was hopelessly unfit to assume the weighty responsibilities of leadership in the church" (*Guard the Gospel*, InterVarsity, p. 19). Then Stott gives three good reasons why Timothy was unfit: (1) He was too young. The word for *youth* in Greek society referred to anyone under 40; later, the Apostolic Canons of the church specified that a man should not be a bishop until he was over 50, the age at which, the Canons averred, you could be sure that "he will be past youthful disorders." Timothy was probably not 35 yet.

(2) He was prone to illness. Paul referred to Timothy's "frequent ailments" (1 Tim. 5:23, NASB). Incidentally, that is one of the most quoted passages regarding Timothy. ("No longer drink water exclusively, but use a little wine for the sake of your stomach.") It tells us very little

about whether total abstinence is God's will for us in the 20th century, but it tells us quite a bit about Timothy in the 1st century.

(3) He was timid by temperament. Patrick Fairbairn, another commentator, called Timothy inclined "more to lean than to lead."

If those things are true, then why in the world would Timothy even have been considered for such a strategic role? Well, I suppose the reason is that God delights in using unlikely people.

Moses knew several reasons why he was unsuited for the task of leading the Israelites. God didn't accept his excuses.

Gideon thought the angel of God had chosen the wrong person; after all, he was just a farm boy.

Jeremiah had some of Timothy's characteristics too. He was too young and he didn't have the right temperament to thunder out messages of doom. God appointed him to the job.

Why does God use such people instead of natural-born leaders? Paul explained it once to the Corinthians: "God chose what is foolish in the world to shame the wise, God chose what is weak in the world to shame the strong, God chose what is low and despised in the world, even things that are not to bring to nothing things that are, so that no human being might boast in the presence of God" (1 Cor. 1:27-29, RSV).

Somewhere in that list of unlikely candidates for a divine appointment, Timothy is included. And, chances are, if you look carefully, you may find yourself included too.

The Ephesian Problem
On the surface, however, the problem in Ephesus did not look too severe. Paul referred to it as "vain babbling,"

"old wives' fables" and "make-believe knowledge." And he mentioned genealogies as if the Christians in Ephesus had just seen a TV preview of *Roots* and were seeking to unearth theirs.

Scholars are not completely agreed on what the spiritual malady of Ephesus was. However, it is known that throughout Judaism at this time, fanciful and elaborate interpretations of the Old Testament were spreading like wildfire. These were highly speculative, depending much more on imagination and allegory than on a reasonable explanation of the Old Testament text. Such interpretations opened the door to any new philosophy that came down the pike.

And since the Ephesians were in a position to hear everything that came along, the Christians were always buzzing, considering how they could fit the latest fad into their eclectic theology. Thus, they spent their time talking, arguing, imagining, and accommodating rather than doing.

In other words, one Ephesian might say to another Ephesian: "You know, Socrates was almost as wise as Solomon."

"Maybe they were related."

"Well, Solomon had 1,000 wives, you know. One of them must surely have come from Greece."

And then they would spend the rest of the afternoon, figuring out the relationship or accommodating Solomon's wisdom to Socrates' philosophy.

Or:

"You know that Greek philosophers tell us that matter is bad and only spirit is good."

"What do the Scriptures say?"

"Well, if you read carefully between the lines, they say the same thing. What did Adam and Eve do that was so bad?"

"They ate the forbidden fruit."

"Exactly. That proves that material things are evil."

Well, you can see how this speculation may have seemed like fun and games. Why did Paul get so worked up about it? After all, these people were using the Bible, weren't they? And weren't they discussing religious matters? What could be so wrong about that?

Very wisely, Leon Morris comments, "It is always easier to get into an argument than to live the Christian life. It is human nature to prefer vigorous discussion to sacrificial living. . . . It is still quite possible to use the Bible not as the source of the divine training that is in faith, but as the starting point for the exposition of our own pet theories. Calling these theories 'Christian,' or 'orthodox,' or 'sound doctrine' does not make them so. For that, there must be a real subjection to what God has revealed" (*Scripture Union Bible Study Book, First Timothy to James,* Eerdmans, p. 4).

The Ephesians were going around in circles with their religious talk and neglecting the bull's-eye in the middle of the target—love (1 Tim. 1:5).

Unfortunately, the Ephesians never hit the bull's-eye. A generation later, when John received the Revelation from Christ (Rev. 1), one of the churches he wrote to was the church at Ephesus. The Ephesians were praised for many things, but they were condemned because they had lost their love.

Where had they lost it? They had apparently lost it in a maze of religious talk. Christians today need to remember the lesson. True spirituality can be lost in the rubble of religious talk, and unfortunately, Christians may not even be aware they have lost it.

A Military Letter

Paul's letter to Timothy has a strange military ring to it,

especially since he was concerned that the Ephesians love more, not less. The main point of the epistle was this: "Timothy, this is your commander speaking. Be a good soldier."

Perhaps, having been chained to Roman soldiers for two years, Paul was more aware of military allusions. But more likely Paul was thinking of himself as a father sending his spiritual son Timothy off to war. Timothy was going to have a battle on his hands and he would need to be prepared for it.

So Paul used words like *fight, war, charge, command*—words that he seldom used in his other epistles.

Look at 1 Timothy 1:18, for instance. You might translate it, "This is the military command I am issuing to you. . . . War a good warfare." The Greek word used for *warfare* implies a long military campaign, not an isolated battle. Timothy's two best weapons, according to Paul, were faith and a good conscience (1 Tim. 1:19). Now they might not seem like much compared with a howitzer and an armored tank; yet for the kind of war that Timothy was waging, they would be more effective.

In his Letter to the Ephesians (Eph. 6:10-17), Paul had mentioned several pieces of spiritual armor that any well-dressed Christian ought to wear. But here Paul mentioned only two pieces: Faith refers to the truth of the Gospel; Timothy was urged to grasp it and not let it go. If one doesn't know what he is fighting for, he will never know if he has won. The other piece of armor is a good conscience, which refers to the inner self in communion with the Spirit. The conscience implies being on good terms with one's inner self, as well as having a smooth working relationship with God.

A strong faith and a good conscience are both vital to

successful soldiering.

And also to successful sailoring. For Paul switched metaphors in the middle of the war (1 Tim. 1:19), referring to some who had allowed their faith to be shipwrecked, because they did not have a "good conscience" as a rudder. They went around in circles and ended on the rocks.

Of course, Paul had just as much experience being shipwrecked as he had living with soldiers, so both figures of speech were appropriate for him.

At this point, Timothy might have said, "OK, I want to be a good soldier. I'd also like to be a good sailor. But how?"

Paul listed at least four things that would help Timothy be a good soldier (1 Tim. 4).

• Avoid the foolish myths that are circulating around Ephesus. Don't spend your time arguing about trivia. Avoid the brushfires. The devil likes to divert your attention from things that count.

Even today this is good advice. Modern cult leaders, like those in ancient Ephesus, are specialists in embroidering on details of Scripture. Whether it's Sun Myung Moon's Unification Church or the Jehovah's Witnesses, cultists divert attention from the major matters by building logical cases on minutiae. If you fight the war on their selection of minutiae, you will soon find that you are fighting on quicksand.

• Keep in shape. I don't know if Timothy went out jogging every morning; Paul didn't knock the practice, for he was obviously concerned about Timothy's physical condition. But his main point was, "Keep in spiritual shape." And that may take even more time and effort than it takes to keep in physical shape.

The Salvation Army used to encourage its officers to engage in regular "knee-drill," a vital aspect of spiritual calisthenics.

• Be an example to the troops. Paul advised, "Let no man despise your youth." In today's society, a man in his mid-30s may be accepted as an up-and-coming executive. In Timothy's day it was different.

If you want to get the feel of Timothy's situation, imagine yourself as a young lieutenant, just graduated from college with an ROTC commission, and presiding over Vietnam veterans alongside a drill sergeant who has served 20 years, half of them in combat.

Now in that situation, imagine the advice coming to that young lieutenant: "Don't let anyone laugh at you because you are young." Well, that's easier said than done.

You don't keep them from "despising your youth" by barking military commands or learning how to cuss a bluer streak than anyone else. The way to do it is by being an example.

Commentator E.F. Scott says, "He was to excel in those very qualities in which youth is wont to be deficient—gravity, prudence, consideration for others, trustworthiness, and mastery over the passions" (*The Pastoral Epistles in the Moffat New Testament Commentary*).

Well, maybe these are problems for youth, but Timothy had been praised in at least two of these areas: consideration for others and trustworthiness, or charity and faith. Paul had told the Philippians that no one cared for them like Timothy. Now if Timothy could develop the same kind of care for the Ephesians that he had developed for the Philippians, he would be the example they needed. His faithfulness was never in question.

• Drill. Keep on practicing and doing the things that you know you should do.

Why are fire drills held in school? Why don't teachers simply pass out a sheet of paper at the beginning of the year explaining the procedure to follow in case of fire? Most students, after all, go through the 12 to 16 years of education without ever encountering a fire in their various schools. They may have wished for the schools to burn down, but fires during school hours are a rarity.

Should we abolish fire drills? Of course not. A drill transforms an exceptional action into a habit. And good habits stand us in good stead when emergency strikes. That's why Paul told Timothy, "Make these things a habit."

Bible study needs to become habitual. We need to be drilled in the Word so that we can be skilled in using the Word. The psalmist said, "Thy Word have I hid in mine heart, that I might not sin against Thee" (Ps. 119:11). Paul spoke of the Word as a sword; it is through drill that one becomes proficient in using it.

But Christians also need to become proficient in love, faithfulness, and purity. Unfortunately, some Christians who are thoroughly drilled in the Word seem to have neglected any drill in love.

A Man of God

Just in case Paul hadn't reminded Timothy to be a good soldier often enough, he said it once again near the close of this epistle (1 Tim. 6:11-12). To get Timothy's attention, Paul called him, "O man of God."

Would you like to be called a man or woman of God? If you were honest, you might respond, "You don't know me very well, do you?" Or, "I think the operator must have given you the wrong number."

But Timothy realized that Paul knew him inside and out. Besides that, Timothy knew that the term "man of God" was used of only a few honored figures in the Old Testament: Moses, David, Elijah, for example. That's select company to be in.

The title wasn't given to men because they necessarily deserved it; rather it was because they had been entrusted by God with a high office or a lofty responsibility. Paul wanted Timothy to know that God had entrusted him with a high office.

A Christian may shirk responsibilities because he doesn't think they are significant. A sense of the divine calling, of being God's man in that particular situation, will shed the proper light on a job.

Timothy was then given three words of instruction: Flee, follow, and fight. (There is a parallel passage in 2 Timothy 2:22 which should be compared with this one.)

1. Flee. Soldiers don't like the word *retreat,* but sometimes strategic retreat on one flank will lead to great victories on another. When Paul advised Timothy to "flee these things" (1 Tim. 6:11) or "flee also youthful lusts" (2 Tim. 2:22), he wasn't talking primarily about such things as *Playboy* magazine or topless bars; he was referring primarily to other battles in which one can lose more by winning than by fleeing.

Paul again warned about the Ephesian penchant for getting into word battles. These are the battles you can win that cause you to lose the war. Yet one-upmanship is always tempting; it may give a sense of prestige and pleasure, but the lusts for prestige and pleasure are what a Christian will want to flee.

Next, Paul talked about the materialism treadmill (Eph. 6). You may win in your struggle to get on top and to put piles of money in the bank, but if that's the sum and substance of your life, you will have lost another war. The lust for power and possessions is best avoided. To win the rat race, you have to be a rat. It's best not to enter the race at all.

2. Follow righteousness. The word *follow* seems rather passive. The Greek word actually implies that one should be in hot pursuit of righteousness. It was in this military sector that Timothy was advised to charge forward.

Americans know much more about the pursuit of happiness than they do about the pursuit of righteousness. The pursuit of happiness for its own sake is one of those lusts to be avoided. Pursuing righteousness brings happiness as a byproduct.

You see, pursuing righteousness means living a life in harmony with God and man. When you are in harmony, you are happy. It's as simple as that. Pursuing righteousness is no namby-pamby phrase, for it also implies giving God what is due to Him and working for justice among men. That is a noble pursuit.

3. Fight the good fight. Some translations render this as an athletic competition rather than a military battle, but the meaning is the same. There's a battle on, and it's Timothy's responsibility to contend for victory.

But why did Paul say, "Fight the good fight"? Are any fights good?

About 450 years earlier, a Greek historian named Thucydides wrote the *History of the Peloponesian War,* and used virtually the same words that Paul uses in this passage. The passage from Thucydides is translated, "We fight for something that is worth fighting for." That makes it a good fight.

It is important for any leader to learn where to expend his energies, so that he will not tire himself fighting battles that aren't worth fighting.

But you say, "I feel so inadequate. How can I ever hope to win?"

"The battle will continue," Paul would respond, "and you must continue to fight. But victory has already been assured, because the King of kings and Lord of lords is on your side."

Fight the good fight with all thy might;
Christ is thy strength and Christ thy right;
Lay hold on life and it shall be
Thy joy and crown eternally.

Faint not nor fear for He is near,
He changeth not and thou art dear.
Only believe and thou shalt see
That Christ is all in all to thee.

11

Stir Up
the Fire

On July 19, A.D. 63, someone struck a match to Rome, in a corner of the Circus Maximus. For six days and seven nights, the fire raged, and then Rome's wooden tenements collapsed like toothpicks and burned to the ground. Sacred shrines and priceless historic buildings were gutted. Ten of the city's fourteen precincts were destroyed. The mood of the populace was described as "hopeless wretchedness."

Nero was emperor. When he came to power 10 years earlier, he was known as a gentle young man, and according to Seneca, "incapable of learning cruelty."

But a year later, he ordered the murder of his brother. In A.D. 59, he had his mother assassinated. In A.D. 62, he divorced his wife and then had her murdered. His two able assistants, who had run the empire for him, could take it no longer. One retired; the other died from unknown causes.

Rome's ashes were still smoldering when rumors started flying. Some testified that they had seen Nero's servants in various parts of the city during the conflagration. They seemed to be stirring up the flames rather than dousing them. Others said that Nero had ordered the blaze started so that he could build some grandiose new monuments to himself in the empty lots. A few months later, when Emperor Nero began to erect the Golden House as a private palace, the rumors could not be denied.

The point is that although no one could make the charge of arson stick, it was embarrassing for the emperor to have to walk around his own city with a cloud of guilt floating above his head.

He would have to find a scapegoat. He would have to find a group of people who were viewed with suspicion by the majority of the population. If it was a growing group, others might feel threatened by it.

The Christian church fit into Nero's scheme perfectly. It was viewed as a secret society; it was growing fast; some outsiders were wondering what *really* went on at its communion services (there was talk about eating flesh and drinking blood), and his predecessor Claudius had once run the Christians out of the city.

So Nero began his "pin-the-blame-on-the-Christians" game. It was probably A.D. 65.

The Roman historian Tacitus fills us in on some details: "To suppress the rumors, he [Nero] falsely charged and cruelly punished those persons who were commonly called Christians. . . . Their deaths were made more cruel by the mockery that accompanied them. Some were covered with the skins of wild beasts and torn to pieces by dogs; others perished on the cross or in the flames; and others again were burned after sunset as torches to light up the darkness. Nero himself granted his gardens for the show."

How magnanimous of him! There is little question that Nero thought the Apostle Paul would be a prize catch.

He had probably not been in Rome at the time of the fire, so it would be a bit harder to establish a strong case against him, but the emperor could find a way. After all, it was Paul who had spread the Christian message from one end of Nero's empire to the other. In his own way, he had lit a match to the empire and the fire that he had ignited would never be extinguished.

A Second Letter to Timothy

About three years elapsed between Paul's first and second letters to Timothy. The first letter was written probably in A.D. 63 from Macedonia. The second was written about A.D. 66 from a prison in Rome. What happened in those three years and specifically how Paul was arrested and taken to Rome is unknown.

It's possible that Paul went to Spain during that time. Clement of Rome, writing in A.D. 96, said that Paul reached "the limit of the West," and about the only place that Clement of Rome could consider to be the limit of the West was Spain, which Paul had wanted to evangelize for a dozen years.

After Spain, he probably revisited Timothy in Ephesus and paid courtesy calls on other churches he had founded in the area.

There is no question where Paul was when he wrote the second letter. He was in a Roman jail. And there was no hired house this time. He was probably in an underground dungeon. A small hole in the ceiling might have been his source of light and air. His cell—damp, dark, and dismally lonely. Because of Nero's maniacal mood, Paul, now about 65, faced certain death.

Where was Timothy? Right where Paul had left him.

Good old Timothy was still plugging away in Ephesus, but it had been an uphill struggle. You can't say he had been a failure there, but you wouldn't write a success story about him either. Problems had gotten worse despite Timothy's efforts. An anti-Paul group was gaining power. Old heresies were in vogue and a wave of persecution was rising.

It may have been in Ephesus, though more likely in nearby Troas, that Paul was arrested and taken to Rome. Timothy may even have witnessed the arrest; Paul spoke of a tearful parting (2 Tim. 1:4).

Then, perhaps three months later, Timothy received his second epistle from Paul, who was asking Timothy to come to Rome as quickly as he could. And he wanted Timothy to stop along the way and bring John Mark with him.

(It's interesting to see whom Paul requested to come to Rome, where Christians were being tortured by a mad emperor: Timothy who struggled with timidity and John Mark who had once walked out on Paul when the going got rough.)

This second epistle is a warm, touching letter. Like the first, it contains references to being a good soldier: "Take your share of suffering as a good soldier," and "I have fought a good fight," for example. But the tone is different. Paul's first letter to Timothy was filled with instructions on how to organize the church in Ephesus. The second letter is full of memories and hopes. The first letter was concerned with the present; the second looks at the past and at the future. The first letter was deeply concerned about the church at Ephesus, the kind of impersonal letter which could have been sent to a church office. But the second letter is warm and personal, and shows Paul's deep concern for Timothy.

Imagine Timothy's mood before he received that second letter. He had good reason to be discouraged. Things had not been going too well for him in Ephesus. Besides that he was ready for a move. He hadn't stayed in one place for 3 years since he had departed from Lystra 15 or 16 years earlier. Who could blame him for thinking this might be a good time to return home to Lystra for a while—at least until things cooled down?

He also had good reason to be apprehensive; the future was not rosy. Timothy had seen Paul arrested many times. But this time had to be different; the political climate in Rome had changed. The Roman government may have been tyrannical at times, but it had always been stable. Not any more. Under Nero, rebellion was seething; the emperor himself was acting like a madman.

What did the future hold? For his friend Paul, the future meant almost certain death. But what about Timothy's own future? And what about the future of Christianity? Together he and Paul had labored for a decade and a half, establishing churches. Now church after church was on the verge of collapse, either because of heresy within or persecution without. Christianity, writes Bishop H.C.G. Moule, "trembled on the verge of annihilation" (*Studies in Second Timothy,* Kregel, p. 18). Yes, there would have been good reason for Timothy to be apprehensive.

This must have been the darkest hour in Timothy's life, and he had seen many dark hours. He must have felt a loneliness descending upon him, and a weight of responsibility that was overwhelming. He must have been tempted to run somewhere and hide, not from Rome as much as from all the pressures that were burdening him. Moule says, "Well might he have been shaken to the root of his faith. He might also have tasted a drop of that last despair which gives us God and wishes that being could cease to be."

Lonely? Yes. But it must have been the feeling of inadequacy that really got to Timothy. Once again—but this time more than ever—he felt the responsibility was too big for him to handle.

He had certainly realized that unless the Lord Jesus returned first, Paul would some day be taken from him in death. Paul had experienced many close calls; Timothy wasn't naive about facing death. But now he realized that Paul's death was imminent, and humanly speaking, the future of Christianity would be up to men like Titus and himself. The younger generation would have to take over. That thought, in itself, must have been overwhelming.

The baton was being passed to him; Paul would be dropping out of the race; and Timothy must have felt as if he would have to run his lap with a wooden leg.

Years before, Paul had told the Ephesian elders of his goal: " . . . if only I may finish the race and complete the task the Lord Jesus has given me" (Acts 20:24, NIV). Now he wrote: "I have finished the race" (2 Tim. 4:7, NIV), and he was passing his authority to Timothy.

How could Timothy possibly take over from Paul? He would feel woefully inadequate. With those feelings, Timothy opened his personal letter from Paul and began to read.

Timothy Reads the Letter

In some of his letters, Paul seemed a bit slow in getting to his major point. But not in this one. Hardly had Timothy begun reading when he must have been struck with this statement: "God hath not given us the spirit of fear; but of power, and of love, and of a sound mind" (2 Tim. 1:7).

"Timothy, are you worried that you are not big enough to fill my job?" Paul seemed to ask. "Remember that there is Someone inside of you who is filling you. The Holy Spirit is not afraid of anything."

Jesus had promised when He left His disciples that He

would send the Holy Spirit to take His place and Jesus called the Holy Spirit "a Comforter." The word in Greek means "One who is called alongside to help"; the word *comforter* in Latin literally means "with strength."

Timothy must have reread that part of the letter a couple times; he must have taken time to mull over the meaning of power, love, and a sound mind. The word for *power* is the Greek word from which we get our word *dynamite*. Timothy might not have felt much like dynamite right then, but Paul was telling him that he had the spirit of dynamite within him.

But the Holy Spirit is not only the spirit of power, He is also the spirit of love. Writing to the Galatians, Paul had put love first on his list of fruit of the Spirit, and John said that love—perfect love—is stronger than fear, for it casts out fear. (See 1 John 4:18.)

Do you think Timothy would have been afraid to go to Rome, as Paul had requested, to visit him in prison? Perhaps, but I think his love for Paul would have cast out that fear. Love, after all, is one of the most powerful of all emotions.

But Timothy also had been given the spirit of a sound mind, or "self-control," as many versions translate the Greek word. Admittedly, the Greek word is a hard one to translate. Others have defined it as "soundmindedness-in-action" or the ability to keep cool when everyone around has panicked.

For the Christian, this isn't as hard as it may seem. Knowing that he has a sovereign Father who has the whole world in His hands, and that he is indwelt by the Holy Spirit of power, he should be able to keep his cool even when he meets Nero face to face.

But none of this is automatic, Paul reminded Timothy. And to help him grasp this, the apostle wrote, "Keep stirring up the fire." (See 2 Tim. 1:6.) "Keep it in full flame.'' I don't know whether Paul was thinking of the rumor that Nero's henchmen had been spreading around the city of Rome, adding fuel to the fire. The point that Paul was making is that what God has given us needs to be used, not neglected; it needs to be stirred up like a fire, not allowed to smolder and die out.

That was probably why Paul had been continually prodding Timothy into bigger roles. Left to himself, Timothy might have let the fire cool. Left to himself, Timothy might have succumbed to his tendencies toward timidity. But God's gifts to him were the gifts of power, love, and a sound mind; now, Paul said, was the time to stir up those gifts.

A Sense of History

Throughout the little letter, Paul conveyed a sense of history. Timothy was part of a Gospel chain; he was a runner in a relay race. What he had been given must be passed along intact to the next generation, even as Paul had passed it along to him.

Timothy's grandmother Lois had passed it along to his mother Eunice and then to Timothy. The Gospel was perhaps like a family heirloom that was being passed along. Timothy was admonished to guard it carefully (1:14). He was then given the responsibility to pass it along to "faithful men, who will be able to teach others also" (2 Tim. 2:1, NASB). Notice that the first qualification in this chain was faithfulness or trustworthiness; then the second was the competence to teach it to others.

Thus, five generations were covered with the Gospel. Timothy's grandmother may have been born 30 years before Christ was born in Bethlehem. Timothy would have been born about 30 years after the birth of Christ. If Timothy would pass the Gospel along to a fourth generation who would be able to pass it along to a fifth, a time span of 150 to 200 years might be covered.

Obviously, Paul was thinking historically. That's something today's parents need to do as well. Whether or not they can point backward to a Christian mother and grandmother as Timothy did, they have a responsibility to look ahead, not only to children but also to grandchildren. And the responsibility is two-fold: to point their children to Jesus Christ as Saviour, and to provide adequate Christian training so that their children can in turn pass along the instruction to their offspring. Evangelizing children isn't enough.

Now I mentioned that Paul stressed the need to pass along the Gospel. I referred to it as something like an heirloom. Actually, Paul referred to it as a treasure put into a safety deposit box and entrusted to Timothy (1 Tim. 6:20; 2 Tim. 1:14). "Guard it," he told Timothy.

But what is it? Maybe you remember the guessing game you used to play as a child. Someone was sent out of the room, and the rest of the children picked an object —perhaps a lamp or a book or a table—to be "it." From then on, "it" was never named, but was only described in vague terms. When the child returned to the room, he tried to guess on the basis of clues.

Christian Authority

Christianity is not meant to be a game in which you guess what "it" is. The treasure which Timothy was to pass along was the Gospel. But in 10 or 15 generations, it might become known as a mysterious "it."

So at this point, Timothy could well ask the question, "I am glad to be reminded that the Holy Spirit is inside of me, and I know it is necessary for you to admonish me to guard the deposit and to pass it along intact to future generations. But when generations 17 and 77 come into the world, how will they know what 'it' is?"

There's another parlor game that kids used to play. After forming a circle, the first child whispered a secret into the ear of his neighbor and the secret was passed along from child to child. By the time the secret had gone in and out of a dozen ears, it was totally distorted. The first child might say, "I like ice cream with peanuts," but the last one would hear, "I like Mike Dean but he's nuts."

How can you be sure what "it" is? How can future generations know? Is there any authority?

Throughout the letter, Paul answered this question in various ways.

1. A statement of belief. "Remember Jesus Christ, risen from the dead, descendant of David" (2 Tim. 2:8, NASB). While not as detailed as the Westminster Confession, or the Baptists' New Hampshire Confession, or even as the Apostles' Creed, many scholars view those few words as a rudimentary statement of belief, a place for Timothy and others who followed him to plant their feet and say, "Here I stand."

Of course, inherent in the statement, "descended from David," is the fact that Jesus Christ is the fulfillment of all the Old Testament Messianic prophecies from Genesis 3:15 to Malachi 4:2. He is the Mighty God (Isa. 9) and the One who was wounded for our transgressions (Isa. 53).

2. A song to sing. Singing has always played a big part in the history of the Christian church. Paul himself, who sang as a captive in the Philippian jail, urged the Colossians to train one another in the Gospel with psalms, hymns, and spiritual songs. Thus, Paul quoted a first-century hymn (2 Tim. 2:11-13) that takes Scripture and applies it to life. It was sort of an early version of "Jesus, I My Cross Have Taken" or "Must Jesus Bear the Cross Alone?"

For more than 400 years, Martin Luther's "A Mighty Fortress Is Our God" has been used to stiffen the spiritual backbone of Christians and to impart some basic Christian teaching. Songs can do that.

3. The Word of God. All creeds and all hymns must be measured against the Word of God itself. This is the authority. This is how you know what "it" is. This is how you know, when the message has been passed around the circle, if the words have become garbled.

Just as the Apostle Peter, in his last epistle, pointed repeatedly to the Scriptures, so did Paul in his final epistle to his spiritual son Timothy.

Early in the epistle, Paul referred to the Word of God as a blueprint or a model to follow. The message was called "sound words" or technically, words to help one become spiritually healthy (2 Tim. 1:13, NASB).

It would have been easy for Paul, as he languished in a Roman cell, to feel that God's truth would perish with him. We certainly have that tendency. Everything hinges on us, we think. If we lose, all is lost. But Paul reminded Timothy that although he was in chains, "God's Word is not bound."

Timothy could have been very discouraged about the problems in Ephesus. It didn't look as if any progress had been made. He had been preaching and teaching for three years with little effect. Aware of his personal limitations, he could easily have gotten himself all tied up in knots. But God's Word is not bound.

It's good to remember that no matter how restricted, inadequate, confined, limited, or shut-in one might feel, God's Word is still dynamite. It cannot be bound. God is its Author and He will not allow it to go out of print.

Stay with the Scriptures

Paul made another important point about the Word of

God. Since it is powerful and authoritative, individuals are frequently tempted to twist it to fit their own purposes. It can be used, as a vicious dog can be trained, to devour any opponent. Then it becomes a personal weapon to be wielded upon any whim.

Timothy understood what that was all about. He had been dealing with professional word-twisters. Though they had specialized in making numerous cloverleaf turns, they still could convince a listener that he was on the thruway. These people had "swerved from the truth" (2 Tim. 2:18, RSV).

Paul said, in effect, "If you are a road-builder preparing the way of the Lord, make sure it is a straight road." That's the apparent meaning of the familiar phrase "rightly dividing the Word of truth" (2 Tim. 2:15). The allusion can be either to a farmer plowing a straight furrow in a field or to a road-builder. The point is, as John Stott says: "The Word of truth is a road. . . . If he cuts the road straight, people will be able to follow and so keep in the way" (*Guard the Gospel,* InterVarsity, p. 106). Those who build roads that lead into detours, dead ends, and gravel pits will be put to shame when Jesus Christ returns.

Some of the Ephesians apparently thought that straight roads were too boring, and so the bypaths that they established meandered along dry river beds. The purpose of a road is to lead to a destination as directly as possible. That's the kind of road that Timothy was to build.

So, Paul wrote, "Study to show yourself approved unto God, a workman who does not need to be ashamed, who cuts a straight line through the gobbledygook and presents God's truth as a direct route." (See 2 Tim. 2:15.)

Throughout the letter, Paul kept returning to this main theme: "Stay close to the Scriptures, Timothy, and you won't have to be frightened by the future." He warned against the tendencies of the "last days" (chap. 3). Then he gave this advice: "But as for you, Timothy, stick with the Word of God. The Word of God was good enough for you as a child in Lystra when you learned it at your mother's knee, and it was good enough for you when I came to town and showed you what it said about how to find salvation. Now, Timothy, it is good enough to help you face the future." (See 2 Tim. 3:14-15.)

But I still feel inadequate, Timothy might have thought. That's what the Word of God is designed to cure. Here is what the various translations say is the purpose of the Scriptures. The Bible will make you "proficient" (MOF), "efficient" (NEB), "perfectly fit" (WMS), "well-prepared" (LB), and "thoroughly equipped" (NIV).

You could well be suspicious about such claims were it not for the fact that Paul explained why the Bible can produce those results. "All Scripture," Paul said, "is inspired by God," (literally, "God-breathed"). That's the reason it is profitable (or useful) for doctrine, reproof, correction, and training in righteousness." (See 3:16-17.)

Doctrine (or teaching) and reproof are concerned primarily with that deposit or treasure that we Christians are to guard. The teaching is the positive side, and the reproof is the negative side. It is only through the Scriptures that false teaching can be exposed.

But Paul went on to remind Timothy that Scripture is also useful for correction and instruction in righteousness. These points refer to moral living. The false teachers of Timothy's day—indeed the false teachers of any day—have a tendency to divorce creed from conduct. But the Scriptures marry the two. Throughout history, some groups have emphasized what a person believes;

others, how a person lives. Some have stressed the mind; others have stressed the actions. Some have promoted creeds; others have promoted deeds. The Bible promotes both. A changed life grows out of changed beliefs. Changed beliefs bring about a new commitment, from which comes a new value structure and then a new lifestyle. Paul told the Corinthians that when a man becomes a new creation in Jesus Christ, all things become new. (See 2 Cor. 5:17.)

So when Paul spoke about the Scriptures being profitable for correction, he was speaking primarily of the changed life. The intent of correction is not to point a finger, but to lend a hand. The psalmist conveyed the idea well when he wrote, "How can a young man keep his way pure? By keeping it according to Thy Word" (Ps. 119:9, NASB).

"Instruction in righteousness" has to be understood as a process. The instruction is not knowledge for its own sake. It is not cramming facts into your head, so that you can become a theological wizard. It is instruction in righteousness. The end product is a changed life. And yet there's more. Paul didn't say, " Instruction in righteousness," period. The purpose of this training in righteousness is that you might help others.

William Barclay says, "The study of the Scriptures must never be selfish; it must never be simply for the good of a man's soul. Any change, any conversion which makes a man think of nothing but the fact that he has been saved is no true change and no true conversion. He must study the Scriptures to make himself useful to God and useful to his fellow man" (*The Letters to Timothy, Titus, and Philemon,* Westminster, p. 232).

Preach the Word

Paul was coming to his final words. Timothy wasn't

aware of it at the time, but what we call the fourth chapter of Paul's second letter to Timothy contains the last thoughts of Paul recorded in Sacred Writ. Yet from the ominous tone of the writing, as well as from Paul's dire circumstances, Timothy must have realized that these words were extremely significant.

It sounded as if Paul were writing a legal document: "I charge you in the presence of God and of Christ Jesus who is to judge the living and the dead at His appearing and His kingdom . . . " (see 2 Tim. 4:1).

The substance, however, is only three words: "Preach the Word."

He expanded on these words to say: "Stay at it in season and out of season: convince, reprove, exhort" (see 4:2). But the core of Paul's concern was that Timothy "preach the Word." Timothy could have told of his experiences with Paul; there must have been scores of exciting experiences that people would have loved to hear over and over again. But the point is that Timothy's commission was to preach the Word, whether people wanted to hear it or not.

From beginning to end, Timothy's life was entwined with the Word of God. John Stott says, "His responsibility is not just to hear it, and to believe and obey what he hears; not just to guard it from every falsification; nor just to suffer for it and continue in it; but to preach it to others" (*Guard the Gospel*).

Paul had previously stressed the public aspect of Timothy's involvement with Scripture: "Till I come, give attendance to reading, to exhortation, to doctrine" (1 Tim. 4:13). These three describe the core of the first-century worship service: reading of the Scriptures; exhorting the congregation on the basis of the text; and teaching or catechizing, which is also based on the Scripture.

Other things were also part of first-century worship: prayer, singing, and the communion service. But Paul stressed to Timothy that Scripture was at the heart of it all.

Paul used three verbs to reemphasize how seriously Scripture should be taken: *give attendance* (1 Tim. 4:13); *meditate* (v. 15); and *take heed* (v. 16).

Even though Timothy was well acquainted with the Old Testament Scriptures, and with both Luke and Paul who were in the process of writing more than half the New Testament, he was still reminded to be a student of the Word.

It's surprising how many people want to be disciples without being students of the Word. A disciple is one who obeys the Lord's invitation: "Follow Me and learn of Me." But how can His words be known except through the Scriptures? Doesn't the Holy Spirit give guidance? Yes, but He guides according to the Scriptures. The Holy Spirit is the Inspirer of Holy Writ, and it is through the Scriptures that He speaks.

We should also be mindful of the fact that there are other spirits which seek to guide us as well. The only way to determine whether or not it is the Holy Spirit directing us is to confirm it through Scripture.

Like Timothy, we too must become totally involved in the Word of God throughout our lives.

The End of the Letter

Closing his letter, Paul told Timothy of his experiences in the Roman jail. It hadn't been easy; he had often felt all alone and forsaken by Christian friends. That's one reason why he wanted Timothy and John Mark to visit him.

Paul had already had a preliminary hearing which had gone surprisingly well. Paul even had had a chance to preach the Word.

When he told Timothy to preach the Word "in season and out of season," he was probably referring to occasions such as he had had before the Roman authorities. To do as Paul did takes readiness; but more than that, it takes an urgent desire to create opportunities to share the Word of God.

Despite the fact that Paul was pleased with the outcome of the first hearing, he had no delusions, for there was little hope of his being released from prison this time.

Winter was coming and he wanted Timothy to come before it got too cold. Paul had already sent Timothy's old friend Tychicus to replace him in Ephesus for a while. Paul wanted Timothy to bring with him the following: John Mark, whom Barnabas had reclaimed and who now was useful to Paul; a warm cloak from Troas, for the dungeon would be damp and frigid; and books and parchments. It's possible that these may have included Paul's citizenship papers, which would have been useful to him in his trial. But it's even more likely that the "books and parchments" included some copies of the Old Testament Scriptures.

For Paul, it was worth asking Timothy to travel 1,000 miles so that he could have the Scriptures to read in prison.

What a fitting way to end a letter which over and over again emphasizes the importance of the Scriptures!

I doubt if Timothy needed much time to pack his bags. He was on his way to Rome already.

The Release of Brother Timothy

If you had started a business, and had invested your blood, sweat, and tears for 20 or 30 years to get it to the place where it is today, would you turn your business over to a person like Timothy when you retired?

Here's the picture that Scripture paints of him:

• Naturally timid and fearful: "If Timothy comes, see to it that he has nothing to fear" (1 Cor. 16:10, NIV).

• Youthful appearing; probably not a take-charge guy: "Let no man slight you because you are a youth" (1 Tim. 4:12, MOF).

• Not in the best of health; probably would miss several days a year because of illness: "Stop drinking only water, and use a little wine because of your stomach and your frequent illnesses" (1 Tim. 5:23, NIV).

• Emotions on the surface; perhaps not the proper bearing for a dignified executive: "Recalling your tears, I long to see you" (2 Tim. 1:4, NIV).

• Doesn't like to take risks; may act too cautiously: "For God did not give us a spirit of timidity, but a spirit of power, of love, and of self-discipline (2 Tim. 1:7,

NIV). And "Do not be ashamed to testify about our Lord, or ashamed of me His prisoner. But join with me in suffering" (2 Tim. 1:8, NIV).

- Not mature enough for the pressures of top responsibility: "Flee the evil desires of youth" (2 Tim. 2:22, NIV).

Well, there you have it. You wouldn't want to throw a huge burden of responsibility upon him, would you? Paul did. Why? Because Paul could see some other qualities in Timothy.

- "Timotheus, my workfellow" (Rom. 16:21).
- "Timotheus, who is my beloved son, and faithful in the Lord" (1 Cor. 4:17).
- "He is doing the Lord's work, as I also am" (1 Cor. 16:10, NASB).
- "I have no one else like him, who takes a genuine interest in your welfare" (Phil. 2:20, NIV).
- "Timothy has proved himself, because as a son with his father he has served with me in the work of the Gospel" (Phil. 2:22, NIV).
- "We sent Timothy . . . God's fellow worker in spreading the Gospel of Christ" (1 Thes. 3:2, NIV).
- "I have been reminded of your sincere faith" (2 Tim. 1:5, NIV).
- "From infancy you have known the Holy Scriptures" (2 Tim. 3:15, NIV).

How do you feel about turning over the family business to him now? Paul put a high premium on faithfulness and stick-to-itiveness. People who turned back really bugged him. Witness his reaction when John Mark quit during his first missionary junket; or remember Demas: "For Demas hath forsaken me, having loved this present world" (2 Tim. 4:10). Speaking of his preliminary trial in Rome, Paul said, "No one came to my support, but everyone deserted me" (2 Tim. 4:16, NIV).

Timothy was not a quitter. He had his faults and his frailties, but he was faithful. And as Paul advised Timothy to train leaders to take his place, he suggested first of all that they be faithful, trustworthy, reliable men.

We live in a day of the short attention span. Most people are either flitters or quitters. But Timothy and those who follow in his train are disciples who stick with it.

Paul had warned Timothy repeatedly that the way wouldn't be easy. Back in Lystra when they first met, Paul had warned Timothy that "much tribulation" lay ahead of them. Timothy couldn't say that he hadn't been warned.

All through Paul's last letter to Timothy are intimations of suffering: "Be thou partaker of the afflictions of the Gospel" (1:8); "Endure hardness, as a good soldier (2:3); "Yes, and all that will live godly in Christ Jesus shall suffer persecution" (3:12); "But watch thou in all things, endure afflictions" (4:5).

But, you say, there is no indication that Timothy himself was ever persecuted. He may have faced unusual pressures and problems; he may have undergone unprecedented dangers and difficulties. But was he ever subjected to the same kind of persecution Paul faced? Paul once catalogued his experiences (and this was nearly 10 years before he wrote the second letter to Timothy from a Roman dungeon).

Five times received I forty stripes save one. Thrice was I beaten with rods, once was I stoned, thrice I suffered shipwreck, a night and a day I have been in the deep; in journeyings often, in perils of waters, in perils of robbers, in perils by mine own countrymen, in perils by the heathen, in perils in the city, in perils in the wilderness, in perils in the sea, in perils among false brethren, in weariness, and painfulness, in watchings often, in hunger and thirst, in fastings often, in cold and nakedness (2 Cor. 11:24-27).

Well, you must remember that Timothy had still not reached his 40th birthday. For Paul, the time of intense persecution began after the age of 45.

Problems lay on the horizon not only for Timothy but also for the entire world. As Paul wrote his two epistles to Timothy, he again reminded his son in the faith that trouble was brewing, a brew that would reach its climax in the apocalyptic end of time.

Paul warned against the Gnostic tendencies which would come to the fore a generation or two after Timothy. Deluded by "deceitful spirits," hypocritical teachers with "seared consciences" would teach that marriage was bad and that eating of certain foods was evil. In other words, any pleasure was sinful; the body itself was God's main mistake. (See 1 Tim. 4, NASB.)

Of course, sex was wrong and so were hot fudge sundaes, as well as pizza. In fact, such teachers would make you feel guilty if you weren't living in the wilderness on a diet of bread and water. And the bread had better be a little stale.

Some people today think that the Apostle Paul had notions like that too. But nothing could be farther from the truth. Paul taught that all God's gifts were to be received with thanksgiving. (See 1 Tim. 4:3.) In the first chapter of Genesis, God the Creator declared that everything He had made was good. In fact, the only thing that God had declared not to be good was the fact that man was all alone. So God decreed that man should live in an institution, the institution of marriage, and within that institution sex could be enjoyed.

Again in his second letter to Timothy, Paul dealt with what was around the corner (chap. 3). As the Holy Spirit gave him insight, Paul saw "perilous times." Man's love would be misdirected, and like an off-target missile, this kind of love could be dangerous. Paul said that men would love themselves and their money more than God. Paul could see inklings of this in the church in Rome, and he knew that whenever this spirit invades the Christian church anywhere, it causes the church to degenerate into an empty shell. The Christian church then becomes conformed to society, and its message, while couched in biblical phraseology, is indistinguishable from the popular culture: Live for yourself; get all you can while you can get it; you only go around once in life, so grab all the gusto you can get.

However, a conforming Christianity will never be a transforming Christianity. Soon all moral values become eroded, and men become, as Paul described them, boasters, proud, blasphemers, disobedient to parents, unthankful, and unholy.

Then, as if to top it all, he added that men would be "lovers of pleasure more than lovers of God" (2 Tim. 3:4). Somehow, when you look at it in that light, it makes the end times seem close at hand.

After reading Paul's letter, Timothy packed his bags. The Bible doesn't indicate whether Timothy headed for Rome, but there is 100 percent agreement among commentators (which is a rare phenomenon) that Timothy would have been headed west before you could say Epaphroditus or Onesiphorus.

His first stop may have been Colossae, where John Mark possibly was (Col. 4:10). Then Timothy and Mark together would have traveled to Troas, to pick up the cloak, the books, and the parchments that Paul had requested (2 Tim. 4:13). From Troas, which had a good port, they could have sailed to Rome or else taken the Egnatian Highway across Macedonia. Paul had asked

Timothy to come before winter, so the season was probably late summer or early fall. Since all navigation on the Mediterranean was discontinued between September 14 and November 11, because of dangerous winds, my guess is that Timothy and John Mark may have walked the whole way, except for short crossings of the Aegean and the Adriatic seas. That would have meant more than 800 miles of walking. And that is a long way even for one who is not hampered by "frequent stomach infirmities" as Timothy was.

Paul's Death

Of course, we don't know if Timothy arrived in Rome before Paul's martyrdom or not. According to tradition, in late A.D. 66 or early A.D. 67, Paul was condemned to death and was taken a few miles outside the city of Rome where he was beheaded. I wouldn't be surprised if Timothy was with Paul to the end. He had been there when Paul was stoned in Lystra and taken outside of the city and left as dead, 20 years earlier. Timothy was no doubt one of the Lystran Christians who had gathered around the supposed corpse at that time, disregarding the consequences of an angry mob. So it isn't too much of a conjecture to think that he may have been outside of the city of Rome on that fateful day when his spiritual father had his coronation day.

Coronation day? Yes, that's right. Paul had just finished writing to Timothy, "I am now ready to be offered, and the time of my departure is at hand. . . . Henceforth there is laid up for me a crown of righteousness, which the Lord, the righteous Judge, shall give me at that day: and not to me only, but unto all them also that love His appearing" (2 Tim. 4:6-8).

Even at the time Paul was writing to Timothy, he recognized that the judges of the Roman tribunal were not righteous judges, but one day he would stand before the Judge who is Righteousness personified.

Ironically, Nero was probably out of town. For nearly two years, from A.D. 66 to early A.D. 68, the emperor was visiting Corinth and Athens. Everyone jokes about Emperor Nero fiddling while Rome burned; during those two years while the empire was collapsing around him, he was singing, dancing, and acting. He went from city to city in Greece competing in local contests. Historian Charles Merivale in his *History of the Romans under the Empire* says, "The exertions of Nero were not confined to playing, singing, and acting. He presented himself also as a charioteer, nor was he ashamed to receive the prize even when he had fallen with car and horses to the ground. Wherever he went he challenged the most famous artists to contend with him, and extorted every prize from every competitor."

Meanwhile back at the ranch in Rome, Nero had asked a commoner named Helius to run the empire for him during his absence. Helius outdid Nero in his cruelty. So it would not have been surprising at all for Paul to have been martyred while Helius was sitting in the emperor's chair.

Timothy's Release

But what about Timothy? There is one more reference to Timothy in the Bible. It is often overlooked because it is at the very end of the Epistle to the Hebrews. In fact, it is practically the only personal reference in this 13-chapter letter: "I want you to know that our brother Timothy has been released. If he arrives soon, I will come with him to see you" (Heb. 13:23, NIV)

It is difficult to deduce very much from this intriguing verse. You see, no one knows for sure who wrote the Epistle to the Hebrews, where the author was when he penned it, or to what city it was mailed. The only contemporary mentioned by name was Timothy, so obviously he knew the author. It is apparent that Timothy was being released from something (no doubt, from prison); there is also a reference to some Italian Christians, and there is general agreement that the epistle was written to a cluster of Jewish Christians between A.D. 64 and A.D. 70.

Biblical scholars today doubt that Hebrews was written by Paul (it's not his style), and so the favorite candidates are Barnabas (an early tradition), Silas, Apollos (that's Martin Luther's choice), and Priscilla and Aquila. A decent case can be made for any of those. Many scholars go along with Origen, the third-century church father, who wrote, "Only God knows for sure."

One thing is quite certain: It was not written to Jewish Christians in Jerusalem. Because of the references to Timothy and Italy, it is mere likely that these Jewish Christians were not in Palestine at all. But where they were we can't be certain.

The city of Rome is the leading contender. After all, it had a Jewish population of 50,000 and its Christian congregations tended to be independent. So it's quite possible that in Rome there would have been a few Jewish Christian congregations that needed the pointed admonitions contained in the Book of Hebrews.

Apparently, those Jewish Christians were hesitant about going all the way with Jesus. They acknowledged Him as Messiah, and yet they still clung to Jewish practices. While they had tasted some of the persecution, they may have been identified with the Jewish community, to escape the full force of Nero's sword. In Rome, Judaism was an accepted religion. For many years Christianity was regarded as a sect of Judaism and was thought of as being under the Jewish umbrella. But as more and more Gentiles came into the fold, the situation changed. Christianity, about the time of Nero, became regarded as a separate religion in its own right, and thus as a new religion it lost the official sanction of the Roman Empire. Were Jewish Christians willing to step across the line, regardless of the cost?

The writer to the Hebrews pointed out the superiority of Jesus to the Old Testament sacrifices and priesthood, and the superiority of the New Covenant to the Old, and he encouraged his readers to step out in faith for Jesus Christ, rather than to take a step back to Judaism.

But What about the Suffering?

Paul told the Jewish Christians to do the following things: First of all, keep your eye on the finish line, and remember that you're not the first person to have problems. (Read Hebrews 11:35-38 to learn about a few anonymous saints who had problems too.)

Second, think of Jesus who endured the Cross with no regard for its shame (Heb. 12:2).

Third, look on hardships as the discipline of God. A father who loves his children disciplines them.

Fourth, don't forget our former leaders (Heb. 13:7).

If this letter was indeed written to Hebrew Christians in Rome, one of their former leaders would have been Paul who had recently been martyred outside the city walls.

Then, fifth, remember that we don't have a permanent home. We're pilgrims and strangers here. So don't get your roots planted too deeply on the soil of this old world (Heb. 13:14).

Rome, the eternal city, had been wracked by flames only a few years earlier; Jerusalem, the mother city, would be razed by Roman soldiers in another year or two.

Jesus too was crucified outside the city gates. He was willing to step over the line for you. Are you willing to step over the line for Him?

The Jewish Christians to whom this letter was written did not know that in another year or two the temple at Jerusalem would be destroyed and the system of sacrifices would disappear. They wouldn't be able to play on both sides then.

And then at the end of the epistle was a reference to Timothy being released from prison. Timothy himself was a splendid example of one who had taken his stand for Jesus, who hadn't been daunted by the fear of suffering, who despite physical frailty was willing to go to jail for his faith.

No one knows how Timothy got in prison. It may have been because of his faithfulness to Paul, who had been condemned by Roman authorities. It may have been that he had accompanied Paul to his martyrdom outside the city, while those Hebrew Christians, who were afraid to identify themselves with him, cowered in their homes.

No one knows why Timothy went to prison, but this much is sure; when he was released, he was going to be doing the same things he always had done. Brother Timothy and the author of the epistle would be coming together to visit those Hebrew Christians. A little solitary confinement couldn't keep Timothy from what he had been commissioned by God to do.

When you think of the stalwarts of faith mentioned in Hebrews as examples to follow, you think of that all-star cast in Hebrews 11: Enoch, Noah, Abraham, Moses, etc.

But I have a notion that when the writer to the Hebrews inserted Timothy's name as the only living person mentioned in the book, it was not simply a last-minute addendum.

I think he may have been saying, "You may have a hard time identifying with those Old Testament giants and their faith, but here's a New Testament brother of rather ordinary stature.

"You know Brother Timothy. You know he has stomach problems. You know he's not the fellow you'd want to go with you on a jungle safari. You know he's just a common fellow like yourself.

"But Brother Timothy has just been released from prison, and he's not afraid to come back for more.

"If Brother Timothy can do it, maybe it's time for you to step outside the city gates for Jesus as well."

According to tradition, Brother Timothy was martyred in Ephesus about 20 years later, during the reign of the Emperor Domitian.